'NOT ALL NUNS MAY DO THIS'

'NOT ALL NUNS MAY DO THIS'

TERESA OF AVILA AND FATHER GRACIÁN—THE STORY OF A HISTORIC FRIENDSHIP

ERIKA LORENZ

TRANSLATED FROM THE GERMAN BY CYPRIAN BLAMIRES OCDS

GRACEWING

«Nicht alle Nonnen dürfen das»
Teresa von Avila und Pater Gracián
Die Geschichte einer großen Begegnung
First published in 1983 by Herder

First published in English in 2012 by
Gracewing
2 Southern Avenue
Leominster
Herefordshire HR6 0QF
United Kingdom
www.gracewing.co.uk

ISBN 978 085244 801 4

Typeset by Gracewing

Cover design by Bernardita Peña Hurtado

CONTENTS

TO THE READER

I LOVE TERESA, so it was natural for me to ask about Jerónimo Gracián, the young priest in whom her heart found such fulfilment. But whenever I asked about him, the answer was always the same: 'Oh! It's a taboo subject!' Teresa's love taboo? Saint and Doctor of the Church?

It was quite a difficult business to locate the works of this priest, but I was in for a surprise when I did so, for I discovered a writer of distinction and an excellent narrator. Shining through his pages for us today moreover is the living gaze of the 'Holy Mother Teresa'. It then dawned on me that direct or indirect references to this priest could be found in almost all the letters and reports that Teresa wrote in her later years.

I have made a comparative study of the texts, the thoughts, and the experience of these two individuals who have been so maligned in their friendship. Where I have translated texts, I have aimed to capture their intended meaning rather than to reproduce archaic expressions word for word. At the same time I have tried to capture the style where it reflects the character of the writer.

This story of a love is also the story of the Order for which both Teresa and Gracián lived. It is a story of sweetness alternating with bitterness and successes with intrigues. Now that the taboo-bogey has all faded into history I can see why this was the man that Teresa loved. The reader will be able to see how two persons who had opted for simplicity and quietness in the service of God found themselves in the midst of drama and tumult, tragedy and comedy. The rivalries of those years created a hostile picture of Father Gracián, a black legend subsequently handed down to posterity by a Chronicler who was a friar of the Order. This judgement seemed irrevocable—and the priest was not the only one damaged. So this book needed to be written to clarify the relevant texts by reading them in their proper context. The tangle of facts and dates and what the individuals concerned wanted to do or were able to do or were thinking to do needed to be presented and interpreted.

Those readers who get to the end of this book may find it leaves them in a thoughtful frame of mind, but perhaps there may be a smile on their faces too.

Erika Lorenz
Hamburg, May 1983

Translator's note

THIS BOOK CONTAINS numerous quotations from works by St Teresa, works by Fr Jerónimo Gracián, and others, but the author did not provide page references.

The quotations from St Teresa have been traced and page references provided to the authoritative English-language texts:

The Collected Works of St Teresa of Avila, edited by K. Kavanaugh OCD and O. Rodriguez OCD, 3 volumes, Washington: ICS Publications 1976/1980/1985.
ABBREVIATION: *CW = Collected Works.*

Quotations from St Teresa's Correspondence have been referenced to *The Letters of Saint Teresa of Jesus,* translated and edited by E. Allison Peers, 2 volumes, London: Burns Oates & Washbourne, 1951.
ABBREVIATION: *Letters = The Letters of Saint Teresa of Jesus.*

Most of the other quotations in the book are from Spanish-language texts (again without any page references from the author) that have not appeared in English translation, and they have not been sourced.

1

TERESA, A MYSTIC IN EVERYDAY LIFE

Teresa the beautiful

TERESA SÁNCHEZ DE Cepeda y Ahumada (Ahumada after her mother) was born in Avila on 28 March 1515. Her father was descended from a family of Jewish converts from Toledo, his second wife—Teresa's mother—from a Castilian noble from Valladolid. Teresa had eleven sisters, of whom only three were children of her father's first wife. In the family history the name 'Ahumada', 'the smoked one', had the ring of Christian heroism: locked into a tower together with his sons in a battle against the Moors, one of her forefathers had set the tower alight rather than surrender. Fortunately they all came out alive, otherwise there would have been no Teresa de Ahumada.

Teresa grew up in a prosperous and cultured environment, of the kind which we would today call 'upper middle class'. Her father engaged in lawsuits over his title of nobility, but ultimately this was a great deal less important than the mental agility and culture which distinguished Spanish Jews like him as key players in economic life and in the practical professions open to the university-trained.

It is true that her father did not pursue any occupation, since this would have been unsuitable for a noble Christian and indeed it was quite out of the question for the son of a person forcibly converted who was obliged to keep on proving his Christian credentials. But he was extremely bright and well-read, and moreover he demonstrated an appreciation of social problems, since he not only treated his servants well but even refused to keep slaves, for he viewed the exploitation of this kind of 'staff' – quite normal at the time – as embodying a grave injustice. He also showed an unfailing concern for the sick and the poor.

Teresa's mother was gentle by nature but bright, as her daughter Teresa wrote – in other words not unlike Teresa herself. Her mother married and died very young, and Teresa saw nothing but affliction in her life—perhaps because of her endless succession of pregnancies. She would seek distraction from her day-to-day suffering by immersing herself in knightly romances, which in those days played the role of our modern-day detective stories. This was an example that her daughter too initially followed, only to reject it later. By contrast Teresa made a point of stressing that her father possessed good books in Spanish, some of which he gave the children to read. Among them there may even have been a copy of the bible in Spanish. Later, after Teresa had become a nun, the reading of bibles in the vernacular was forbidden, but Teresa could still quote the Scriptures freely in her books. She either relied on her memory or resorted to what she found in the plethora of spiritual books in circulation, which were frequently larded with bible passages in the vernacular. Furthermore the readings in the daily masses were translated by the priests.

But her father was also concerned about a good 'sporting' education for his children. Teresa was an excellent rider and she delighted in dancing and other social pleasures, for she was naturally full of zest for life and socially at ease.

She would later frequently lament her frivolous contacts with numerous cousins of both sexes, her pleasure in jewellery, clothes, and hairstyles, and indeed her own beauty and popularity. From the start it was her instinctive aim to make herself popular, and underneath this may have lurked a yearning for love in the face of the danger of being submerged in her huge extended family. Moreover there was the fact that at fourteen she had already lost her mother.

Father Gracián, her partner in this book, later wrote of her:

> The beauty of Teresa was enhanced and enriched by her humility and her striving for perfection'. In Platonic style he identifies the beautiful with the good here, but he also says still more concretely: 'She had such beauty of disposition and character, she was so friendly, gentle, and charming, that she drew to her all those with whom she mixed, since she loved and treasured them. She felt repelled by the rough and extreme ways to be found in the lives of a few saints, ways which seemed repugnant to herself and to others.

Father Gracián compares her with Joseph the son of Jacob, as depicted in the Book of Genesis:

> They talked about Joseph's beautiful face, and the women of the town gathering together to see his beauty when he went outside of the gate. Our Teresa was pleasing to God, to the angels,

to the saints and to all those who knew her. She
received from God all the blessings of heaven
and earth, for the Lord gave her great natural
gifts—blessings of the earth, along with supernatural graces and talents—blessings of heaven.

The blessings of earth and heaven were visible from
her early childhood. As a child, Teresa revealed her
leaning to the life of the cloister first in her play and
then more clearly in the indelible impression made on
her by the word 'eternity'. She repeated it rhythmically
as if it were a mantra or the Russian prayer of the heart.
Teresa was so deeply affected by the depth of this
word that she got together with her brother Rodrigo
in an act of Christian heroism, whereby as a seven-year
old she set out to fight against the Moors and to suffer
martyrdom for Christ and for his eternity. Fortunately
this 'children's crusade' ended safe and well on the
other side of the stern old walls of Avila, where a
concerned uncle picked up the runaways.

After her mother's death Teresa boarded for a short
period (ended by illness) with the Augustinian canon-
esses, and this experience of the religious life may have
influenced her decision – first taken at the age of 21
and against her father's wishes—to enter the Carmelite
'Monastery of the Incarnation' (*Convento de Nuestra
Señora de la Encarnación*) in Avila. After entering she
again went down with a serious illness, and these two
episodes of sickness may have been symptomatic of
the presence of inner conflicts.

Teresa herself cites as the main reason for her entry
into the life of the cloister 'a miserable fear' of hell,
something which had penetrated into her conscious-
ness through her preoccupation with the word 'eter-

nity'. At the same time the fact that one of her friends was in this convent must have been an inducement.

It might be supposed that there were still deeper and more fundamental reasons not mentioned by the saint. She herself reports the great graces which she immediately received in her first days in the convent. By this she meant experiences of God, inner experiences, to which she was predisposed in a unique way. She thought that God had given her a comprehensive instantaneous foretaste of everything that was to unfold gradually over many years in her later spiritual life.

Before her entry into the monastery on 2 November 1535 Teresa had contemplated marriage, having in mind a much-loved cousin, although she makes no mention of her opting for monastic life being complicated by inner struggles or obstacles. Nonetheless, in terms of the conditions of the day she was already an 'old maid' by the time she decided to enter monastic life. Her mother had married at fourteen and the Franciscan Osuna—who was highly prized by Teresa—labelled a man of forty as a 'worthy old man'. The judgement of what constitutes 'young' has changed over the centuries. This makes Teresa's regrets about how slow she was to pay fully serious attention to God and the love of God much more comprehensible. She writes in her *Life*:

> … neither did I enjoy God nor did I find happiness in the world. When I was experiencing the enjoyments of the world, I felt sorrow when I recalled what I owed to God. When I was with God, my attachments to the world disturbed me. This is a war so troublesome that I don't

know how I was able to suffer it even a month,
much less for so many years.[1]

God's compassion

As sincerely and truly felt as these statements are, there
is also another circumstance to be pondered: In 1560-
1562 Teresa wrote her *Life* (the first significant autobiography with a literary dimension in Spain), making
connections with St Augustine's *Confessions* and clearly
following his example. About her first encounter with
the famous book in the year 1554 she reported:

> At this time they gave me *The Confessions of St
> Augustine*. It seems the Lord ordained this,
> because I had not tried to procure a copy, nor
> had I ever seen one. I am very fond of St
> Augustine, because the convent where I stayed
> as a lay person belonged to his order; and also
> because he had been a sinner, for I found great
> consolation in sinners whom, after having been
> sinners, the Lord brought back to himself. It
> seemed to me that I could find help in them and
> that since the Lord had pardoned them He
> could also pardon me. But there was one thing
> that left me inconsolable, as I have mentioned,
> and that was that the Lord called them only
> once, and they did not turn back and fall again;
> whereas in my case I had turned back so often
> that I was worn out from it. But by considering
> the love He bore me, I regained my courage, for
> I never lost confidence in His mercy; in myself,
> I lost it many times.[2]

The saint not only considers the 'tone' of Augustine
here, she also assimilates his basic attitude in the
composition of her own account of her life: the person
Teresa must be represented in all her sinfulness and

worthlessness, so that God's almighty compassion may be glorified. For that is the real meaning of this *Life*: first and foremost it is about God's love for Teresa as an unworthy channel of that love. Augustine's book begins:

> Great art Thou, O Lord, and greatly to be praised; great is Thy power, and Thy wisdom infinite. And Thee would man praise; man, but a particle of Thy creation, man, that bears about him his mortality, the witness of his sin, the witness that Thou resisteth the proud; yet would man praise Thee; he, but a particle of Thy creation. Thou awakest us to delight in Thy praise; for thou madest us for Thyself, and our heart is restless, until it repose in thee[3].

St Teresa once wrote:

> Though I see clearly that it will be to no one's liking to see something so wretched, not without cause have I dwelt at such length on this period in my life. For I certainly wish that those who read this would abhor me when they see a soul so pertinacious and ungrateful towards Him who bestowed on her so many favours... I voyaged on this tempestuous sea... in a life so beneath perfection that I paid almost no attention to venial sins. And mortal sins, although I feared them, I did not fear them as I should have since I did not turn away from the dangers... However, I see clearly the great mercy the Lord bestowed on me; for though I continued to associate with the world, I had the courage to practice prayer.[4]

Teresa, who has also been called a 'genius at friendship', draws from God's 'nevertheless' conclusions that are developed on the foundation of Christian teaching even though they are also very personal to her:

> I saw that God is also truly man and He is not horrified by our weaknesses, but understands our wretchedness, our constitution subject to original sin, from inside. That is why He came into the world for our redemption. We can associate with Him as with a friend, however much He still remains the Lord... O you my Lord and God! We stand really stunned before your majestic glory, but yet your humility makes us even more stunned, my Lord, at the love with which you greet anybody like me.[5]

There is a correspondence between Augustine's religious feel for life and the womanliness and the sheer reality of Teresa's nature. In other words, what she writes is simply her inner truth, she has no thought of creating literature 'on the side'. Father Jerónimo Gracián, who knew her better than anyone, did not see in her the legendary boyish Amazon of the traditional accounts, which reflected the impression made by her immense activity in laying the foundations of the Reform. He reports:

> The Lord ordained that his servant [Teresa] should be very humble. She was also timid and lacking in self-confidence and faith in her great talent, to a degree that I have never encountered in any others of my female penitents.

Her insecurity was not diminished by her entry into the life of the cloister: indeed it actually increased, for in those days the Carmelite Monastery of the Incarnation in Avila still resembled a home for pious gentlewomen—a '*Beatario*' as such an institution was called in Spain—out of which it had indeed emerged. There was as yet no regular female Carmelite Order in that country—it was Teresa who first set one up. The 180 nuns of the 'Convent of Our Lady of the Incarnation' were not bound to any enclosure, they had servants, and they received frequent visits. So insofar as she was not hindered by illnesses, Teresa's life in the cloister was lived largely in the parlour. The whole of Avila took pleasure in the lively kindness of this 'Lady Carmelite', who was still known as Doña Teresa de Ahumada. Why had she chosen this particular convent? Along with the presence there of the friend we heard about earlier, other reasons can be suggested: on the death of her mother Teresa had asked the Mother of God to take her as her daughter, and the Carmelite Order was dedicated to the Mother of God. Furthermore, the Order looked back to remote eremitical origins on Mount Carmel in Palestine: and early on when she was still a child Teresa had shown an inclination for this contemplative form of life, even though it seemed to run contrary to her so-called 'extrovertness'. Perhaps it was just this kind of widening of horizons that she needed to attain to a harmonious inner development. For all that it took her time to find her way of contemplative prayer, she was undoubtedly gifted for it, or, as we would say today, endowed with a genius for this kind of spiritual life.

The new house

All the superficiality and half-heartedness which Teresa herself repeatedly lamented was then not merely encouraged from outside but was in fact mandatory. And it required a deep inner upheaval for Teresa, a seeker—but one somewhat lacking in self-

confidence — to find her own way to founding monasteries and reforming the Order. As was to be so often
the case in her life, it was a profound visual and
emotional experience that brought about the inner
transformation.

> Well, my soul was now tired; and, in spite of its
> desire, my wretched habits would not allow it
> rest. It happened to me that one day entering
> the oratory I saw a statue they had borrowed
> for a certain feast to be celebrated in the house.
> It represented the much wounded Christ and
> was very devotional so that beholding it I was
> utterly distressed in seeing Him that way, for it
> well represented what He suffered for us. I felt
> so keenly aware of how poorly I thanked Him
> for those wounds that, it seems to me, my heart
> broke. Beseeching Him to strengthen me once
> and for all that I might not offend Him, I threw
> myself down before Him with the greatest
> outpouring of tears.
>
> I was very devoted to the glorious Magdalene
> and frequently thought about her conversion,
> especially when I received Communion. For
> since I knew the Lord was certainly present
> there within me, I, thinking that He would not
> despise my tears, placed myself at his feet. And
> I didn't know what I was saying (He did a great
> deal who allowed me to shed them for Him,
> since I so quickly forgot that sentiment); and I
> commended myself to this glorious saint that
> she might obtain pardon for me.
>
> But in this latter instance with this statue I am
> speaking of, it seems to me I profited more, for
> I was very distrustful of myself and placed all
> my trust in God. I think I then said that I would

not rise from there until He granted what I was begging Him for. I believe certainly this was beneficial to me, because from that time I went on improving.[6]

This rapid advance, founded in a newly acquired trust in God, had two kinds of consequences. Firstly, Teresa found a way of inner contemplative prayer that was both sure and also up to a certain point teachable, and secondly, she could put into practice her huge decision to found a monastery and reform the Order. She felt supported in this by the inner call of 'His Majesty' God, but immediately she sensed the first hint of opposition from within the Order and out in the wider world.

I sometimes reflect that … I was terribly wicked. [but] …

I was thinking about what I could do for God, and I thought that the first thing was to follow the call to the religious life, which His Majesty had given me, by keeping my rule as perfectly as I could. Even though there were many servants of God in the house where I was, and He was very well served in it, the nuns because of great necessity often went out to places where they could stay – with the decorum proper to religious. Also, the rule was not kept in its prime rigor, but was observed the way it was in the whole order, that is, according to the bull of mitigation. There were also other disadvantages; it seemed to me that the monastery had a lot of comfort since it was a large and pleasant one….

It happened once while I was with someone that she mentioned to me and to the others in the group that if we couldn't be nuns like the discalced, it would still be possible to found a monastery. Since I was having these desires, I began to discuss the matter ... I was still delaying.

One day after Communion, His majesty earnestly commanded me to strive for this new monastery with all my powers, ...

This vision had such great effects, and this locution the Lord granted was of such a nature, that I couldn't doubt it was from God...

Hardly had the knowledge of it begun to spread throughout the city when the great persecution that cannot be briefly described came upon us: gossip, derision, saying that it was foolishness. As for me, they said I was well off in my own monastery ...

His Majesty began to console and encourage me. He told me that in this I would see what the saints who had founded religious orders had suffered, that I would have to suffer much more persecution than I could imagine, and that we shouldn't let it bother us...

especially in my case, it was painful to see the provincial opposed to it; had he accepted it, I'd have been excused by all...

Yet, as I say, I thought it would be impossible to give up the project. I believed that since it didn't go against Sacred Scripture or against the laws of the Church, which we were obliged to keep, the revelation was true...

Being at this juncture, always having the help of many prayers, and having already bought the house in a good section, I didn't worry about it being small.[7]

However, until the monastery could actually be consecrated, Teresa still had to battle against endless intrigues and enmities. Although she did so with intelligent resourcefulness, she often felt at the end of her abilities and her strength. Then she said: 'Lord, this house is not mine; it was founded for You; now that there is no one to take care of its affairs, You, Your Majesty, must do so.'[8]

In the knowledge that she had a task from God the saint, now known as Teresa of Jesus, adopted a strategy that was anything but timid. In spite of her fragile health, she went on to found eleven monasteries in the space of thirteen years, i. e. up to 1575 — in Avila, Medina del Campo, Malagón, Valladolid, Toledo, Pastrana, Salamanca, Alba de Tormes, Segovia, Beas de Segura, and Seville. Of the foundation in Seville she reported:

> Well, when we arrived at the house which, as I say, they had rented for us, I thought we could immediately take possession, as was my custom, so that we could say the Divine Office. But Father Mariano began to procrastinate – he was the one who was there – and so as not to cause me any grief, he did not want to tell me everything. Since he didn't have sufficient reasons, I understood where the difficulty lay, which was that the license had not been granted.[9]

At the cost of huge efforts and surmounting great difficulties, Teresa managed to obtain the requisite permission, only to find that the existing inmates of the House tried to ignore her, so she took a gamble and led a 'squat' there:

> What we had to go through before moving in was no trifle. The occupant did not want to leave, and the Franciscan friars, since they were nearby, came at once trying to persuade us that we should by no means move in. If the contract had not been firmly signed, I would have praised God that it could be broken …

> This trouble lasted more than a month. God was finally pleased that we move, the prioress with myself and two other nuns, in great fear, at night so that the friars would not be aware until we took possession. Those who came with us said that every shadow they saw seemed to be a friar. When morning came, the good Garciál-varez, who was with us, said the first Mass, and then our fears left us.[10]

The obstacles had been massive: on the way to Seville the wheels of their wagon ran into a sandbank in the Guadalquivir River (at the town of Espeluy). The foundress depicts the scene with dramatic force:

> … they had to wind their way across: the rope from the other shore was of some help by flowing with the barge. However, it happened that those who were holding the rope let it go, or I don't know what happened, for the barge went off with the wagon and without rope or oars. I felt much more concern in seeing the anxiety of the boatman than I did about the danger. We were all praying; the others were all screaming.

> A gentleman watching us from a nearby castle was moved with pity and sent someone to help,

for the barge then had not yet broken loose and our brothers were pulling, using all their strength; but the force of the water dragged them along to the point that some fell to the ground...

But as His Majesty always gives trials in a compassionate way, so He did here. It happened that the boat got stuck on part of a sand bar where there was not much water; thus a rescue was made possible. Since nightfall had come, we would not have known how to continue our journey if someone from the castle had not come to guide us.[11]

But the difficulties did not end there: at Córdoba the wagons had to stop at the bridge, because permission had not been granted for a crossing, but then, even worse, they got stuck on the bridge because the wagon coverings were higher than the bridge gate. Teresa insisted on these covered wagons, for they enabled her to preserve some kind of rudimentary enclosure. So the upper part of the bridge gate had to be cut off to enable the wagons to pass under. All in all, their entry into Córdoba cannot be said to have gone unnoticed, and Teresa, who was suffering from a fever, relates with humorous irony:

We got out near the church, and although no one was able to see our faces, since we always wore large veils in front of them, it was enough for the people to see us with the veils, the white, coarse woollen mantles we wore, and our sandals of hemp for them to get all stirred up; and that's what happened. The shock was certainly a great one for me and for all, and it must have taken away my fever completely...

> From the uproar of the people you would think
> that a herd of bulls had come into the church.[12]

This very realistic side of the saint's character also
shows through in her letters. For example, a mention
of a Moorish uprising in Seville occurs alongside a
recommendation for the use of mature rose-hips as a
cure for bladder complaints. On other occasions she
shares her recipes for marmalade and offers advice for
avoiding chilblains, or writes to a 'dear honoured
lady', to suggest that she should for the sake of God
and Teresa go to confession frequently, and this
followed by a postscript: 'Yes, please send me some
turkeys, since you have so many'.[13]

Martha and Mary

These robustly realistic remarks should not however
allow us to forget that Teresa was a mystic, for indeed
at the deepest level they were connected to her prayer
life. Teresa managed to resolve the conflict in the
Christian life that so frequently recurs between the
active and the contemplative life, between 'Martha'
and 'Mary':

> ... Martha and Mary never fail to work almost
> together... For in the active—and seemingly
> exterior—work the soul is working interiorly.
> And when the active works rise from this
> interior root, they become lovely and very
> fragrant flowers. For they proceed from this tree
> of God's love and are done for Him alone,
> without any self-interest. The fragrance from
> these flowers spreads to the benefit of many. It
> is a fragrance that lasts, not passing quickly, but
> having great effect.[14]

Ultimately she undertook foundations and reforms not for the sake of the Order, but for the sake of God and her unbelieving fellow humans. The Protestant schisms in Europe moved her no less than the salvation of the souls of the numberless Indians in America (discovered in 1492), from where her beloved brother Lorenzo, who had emigrated to Peru, sent her graphic reports. She wrote:

> It seemed to me that I would have given a thousand lives to save one soul out of the many that were being lost there. I realized I was a woman and wretched and incapable of doing any of the useful things I desired to do in the service of the Lord ... I resolved to do the little that was in my power; that is, to follow the evangelical counsels as perfectly as I could and strive that these few persons who live here do the same. I did this trusting in the great goodness of God, who never fails to help anyone who is determined to give up everything for Him.[15]

The directions Teresa received at decisive points in her life from visions demonstrate the strength of the mystical underpinning to all this. She carefully dated her entry into the *Unio mystica*, the essentially divine-human harmony of loving and willing, by reference to a vision:

> While at the Incarnation in the second year that I was prioress, on the octave of the feast of St Martin (November 1572) ...

> He appeared to me in an imaginative vision, as at other times, very interiorly, and He gave me His right hand and said: 'Behold this nail; it is a sign you will be bride from today on ...'

> This favour produced such an effect in me I
> couldn't contain myself, and I remained as
> though entranced. I asked the Lord either to
> raise me from my lowliness or not grant me
> such a favour; for it didn't seem to me my
> nature could bear it.[16]

Teresa was very well aware of the awkwardness of her
visionary disposition. That is why she went one day,
as Father Gracián reports, to the Inquisitor Francisco
de Salazar, subsequently Bishop of Salamanca, and
said to him:

> My Lord, through the way I pray I often have
> unusual spiritual experiences such as ecstasies,
> raptures, and revelations. But I would like to be
> sure that I am not being tricked by the Devil. So
> I am placing myself in the hands of the Holy
> Inquisition, so that they may examine the state
> of my soul and my way of prayer. I will abide
> by all their instructions.

To this the Inquisitor replied:

> My Lady, the Inquisition does not concern itself
> with examining the state of people's souls or
> their ways of proceeding in prayer. It has the
> task of punishing heretics. Write a plain and
> truthful account of all these things that take
> place in you interiorly and send the document
> to Father Master Juan de Avila, who is a knowl-
> edgeable man with much experience of these
> prayer matters. You can have complete confi-
> dence in his reply.

This suggestion by the Inquisitor was the first stimulus
for Teresa to write down her life story, which brings
her personality so timelessly near to us. Father Gracián
saw the uniqueness of Teresa, and likewise the essence

of the reformed Order, in a balance between missionary activity and mystical experience. He traced this
back to the 'origin' of the Order in the task and life of
the Old Testament prophet Elijah of Mount Carmel:

> He embraced both aims equally, zeal for
> mission and the peace of the Spirit; preaching
> and the ascetic life, love for God and love for
> our neighbour, prayer and spiritual direction.
>
> It was the task of the followers of Elijah to win
> many souls for God, and convert unbelievers,
> heathens, and sinners, while defending the
> Catholic Church against heresies.

It was incumbent on men, wrote Gracián, to do missionary work not with the sword but through knowledge and the power of persuasion, while women had
to work 'through prayer and the example of their
hallowed life'—both of which he saw exemplified in
Mother Teresa, for—as he explained after her death—
she possessed all the virtues, combined to a degree
almost without precedent in a single individual.

> Virtue always implies moderation, and
> extremes of mortification become vices: pen-
> ance, for example is a virtue but only when it is
> implemented moderately and reasonably, oth-
> erwise it culpably damages health. So it is with
> the other virtues. I have never seen so much
> moderation and order as in Holy Mother
> Teresa, both in thinking and in action, in being
> and in speaking. As ardently, passionately and
> devotedly as she served God, she yet possessed
> a sense of proportion and sound instincts. She
> carried out everything in well ordered fashion
> and discreetly with exceptional prudence, after
> she had thoroughly informed herself and taken

advice in order to be quite sure of what she was
doing. Only in love for God, which knows
neither measure nor limits, as we read in Ezra,
did she give her spirit full rein, lighting a flame
in her heart that was not hidden but set on a
lampstand, so as to give light to all. She was full
of zeal for mission, however much it may have
been moderated through contemplation and
inner composure. She led and taught a hard
ascetic life, but her demands on her daughters
were laced with compassion so that nothing
was out of kilter. It was on the basis of a
balanced life lived in strength and blessedness
that she was able to found her well-ordered
monasteries.

This servant of God seems like Isaiah to have
gazed on the glory of the throne of God, on both
sides of which the Seraphim praise God cease-
lessly with the cry: 'Holy, Holy, Holy is the God
of hosts!' (Is 6, 2-3). But Teresa combined two
contradictory sides: she neglected none of the
many duties and labours which were imposed
on her by the task of founding monasteries and
the direction of the nuns, yet she always turned
up on time in the chapel for the hours of prayer
and communal praise of God. Teresa was a
deeply spiritual soul who lived constantly in
the presence of God. She revealed and glorified
this presence as she travelled tirelessly and
made her foundations, carried on negotiations
and established relationships, all so that many
souls might be won for God. We can quite
rightly call the Holy Mother Teresa a queen, for
her spirit was so great and queenly and only
directed to that which concerned God: she
disregarded everything petty and instead of

being anxious she bore before the world the
banner of the cross of the discipleship of Christ.

Again and again we find that the complex figure of St
Teresa of Avila can be grasped only in contradiction
and paradox—something she has in common with
God. By the time Father Gracián got to know her she
was already living in *Unio mystica*, so her love knew
no bounds. This saint understood love for God and
love for man as inseparable unity:

> We cannot know whether or not we love God,
> although there are strong indications for recog-
> nising that we do love Him; but we can know
> whether we love our neighbour. And be certain
> that the more advanced you see you are in love
> for your neighbour the more advanced you will
> be in the love of God… we will not reach
> perfection in the love of neighbour if that love
> doesn't rise from love of God as its root.[17]

A great Teresa specialist of today, Otger Steggink
O.Carm., considers that her significance for our time
lies in what she teaches us about the 'harmony
between the affective and the spiritual life'. He
observes that she continues to be 'a living challenge
for biographers, psychologists, and theologians'.

Notes

[1] *Life* in *CW* i, 66.
[2] *Life* in *CW* i, 72.
[3] Translation retrieved from the Internet.
[4] *Life* in *CW* i, 65–66.
[5] *Life* in *CW* i, 37, 5, 6.
[6] *Life* ch. 9, i-iii in *CW* i, 70.
[7] *Life* ch. 32, vii/ix/x in *CW* i, 215.
[8] *Life* ch. 36, xvii in *CW* i, 247.

9   *Foundations* ch. 24, xvi in *CW* iii, 228.
10 *Foundations* ch. 25, vi/vii in *CW* iii, 232.
11 *Foundations* ch. 24, x/xi in *CW* iii, 225.
12 *Foundations* ch. 24, xiii/xiv in *CW* iii, 226.
13 Quotation not found.
14 *Meditations on the Song of Songs* ch. 7, ii in *CW* ii, 257.
15 *Way of Perfection* ch. 1, ii in *CW* ii, 41.
16 *Spiritual Testimonies* 31 in *CW* i, 336.
17 *Interior Castle* v, 8/9 in *CW* ii, 351.

2

THE PRIEST LOVED BY ALL

Early days

HE TOWN OF Valladolid, in which Jerónimo Gracián first saw the light of this world on 6 June 1545, was at that time the seat of the Spanish Court. The great empire of Charles V and Philip II, on which the sun never set, made for a somewhat restless environment; Valladolid was followed by Toledo, and then Madrid only became the capital in 1561. The Gracián family, which had held significant offices at the royal court for two generations, therefore had to move house several times. Jerónimo's father was Don Diego Gracián de Alderete, highly educated in the Humanities and also known as a writer and a translator of Classical literature. He was a secretary and interpreter under both kings, for their knowledge of languages did not correspond to the extent of their empire. Don Diego mastered Latin, Greek, and Arabic as well as French, German, and English. He seems not to have been secretary in the eminently political sense of his notorious 'colleague' Antonio Pérez, i.e. less a secretary of state than a scholar busying himself with the official documents of the 'prudent king', whose prudence was not apparent in the financial management of his state. For all his lively interest in women, the King was a rather introverted and scholarly type. He pressed on with the great unified 'Empire ideal' of the Catholic monarchs and so felt himself obliged to defend this now hugely enlarged empire both against Islam and against emergent Protestantism.

The young Jerónimo grew up in this atmosphere of struggle against the 'unbelievers', and he developed such a strong 'apostolic' sense that—for all his famously peaceable nature—he became the first to send Carmelite missionaries to Africa and America.

It would take him a very long journey to reach that point, but the openness to the world he would display may have been enhanced by his mother's influence as well as by his father's. She was the daughter of the Polish Ambassador to the Spanish Court and a relative of the King of Poland, Sigismund I. Her name 'Danzick' was Hispanicised to 'Dantisco'. Doña Juana was only twelve when she married, and her husband was originally called not Gracián but García. Since García is as common in Spain as Smith in England, his fellow students at the University of Louvain, where he distinguished himself at classical languages, preferred to call him Gratianus, which then translated to Gracián in Spanish.

The couple had so many children and Juana was married so young that the information provided by different biographers as to their offspring varies—and all we can be sure of is that thirteen of these children remained alive long enough to be worth mentioning.

Five of them went into the monasteries of the Teresian reform, including the most gifted of the whole flock, Jerónimo. Antonio, the eldest, served King Philip as secretary from 1571 to 1576 like his father. He died all too young and was later replaced by Tomás, whom literary history has often mixed up with Lucás. Lucás was a truly romantic figure, a well-known poet and magician in Toledo and the slim and melancholy-looking unknown figure in the paintings of El Greco, who had chosen Toledo as his home.

The prudent Jerónimo was originally chosen by his father to be his successor at Court as royal secretary. His father taught him the art of writing, the beautiful flourish of penmanship, the refinements of letter-writing style, and the drafting of legal documents and deeds with their abbreviations and their curlicues. At the age of ten the lad also began the study of rhetoric and grammar together with classical languages in Valladolid. He then took up the study of philosophy in Toledo, and at 15 he enrolled as a student at Spain's famous Humanist University of Alcalá de Henares. Here he shone in the '*Artes*' and so he was able to get some tutoring work from time to time. His strong inclination for the religious life led him to hold preliminary conversations with the Society of Jesus about becoming a member. The Jesuits' response to his inquiry was very positive. Gracián graduated shortly afterwards in brilliant fashion but this turned his thoughts back to more worldly considerations, and he developed a growing interest in the career of a university teacher. He threw himself energetically into his studies and gained his Licentiate with distinction and finally his Master's degree—but he also damaged his health, and at the age of 19 had to break off his studies.

He was however by no means an unappealingly geekish type. His peers loved him, and although his huge intelligence combined with a phenomenal memory allowed him to absorb the syllabus with spectacular ease, he lost none of his joyously gentle and almost childlike charm.

His illness actually helped him to win his father over to his heart's desire—theological studies. His hope was that later he could make use of his gifts and inclinations as priest and university teacher. On 25 March 1570 he was ordained to the priesthood. But his studies continued, for in order to be able to obtain a teaching position he needed a doctorate. He found himself increasingly immersed in the history of the Carmelite Order, which he planned to take as the subject of the last phase of his doctoral exams. But he was never to bring his studies to their conclusion, for the fascination of the Order that Mother Teresa of Jesus was just then in process of renewing proved stronger than all his career plans.

Gracián himself relates how this came about through providential events which initially looked like minor mistakes. As a young priest he wanted to go to Alcalá on the Feast of St Francis of Assisi to say Mass with the Franciscan Sisters. But he had got the time wrong, so he went instead into the nearby '*De la Concepción*' convent whose inmates he mistakenly believed also to be Franciscans. He proceeded to preach a fine sermon about their charism. Preaching that combined good sense with the power to move his hearers was to become his strength all his life. It was only when the Prioress invited him into the Parlour afterwards that it became apparent to him that he had actually been speaking to Discalced Carmelites—of a kind at least, for the energetic and strict Prioress María de Jésus had founded the convent on her own initiative. Only later did she request statutes from Mother Teresa of Jesus, who was none too happy about it, for the Prioress of Alcalá gave the statutes a very idiosyncratic interpretation. None of this however was of concern to the young priest. He tells us:

After Mass the Mother Prioress asked me if in the future I could hear the confessions of herself and of the other sisters too if they so desired. In order to be able to fulfil this request properly, I asked her to give me a copy of the rules of the convent. She gave me the one that had been written by Mother Teresa of Jesus. This was the first time I had heard of her. I liked her statutes so much that I made notes and quickly wrote down a few thoughts which occurred to me with regard to them from the Holy Scriptures on the life of the foundation prophets Elijah and Elishah. I sent this little piece in a letter to Mother Teresa of Jesus, who was not as yet personally known to me, and I received a letter of thanks from her. I believe it was her prayer that impelled me soon afterwards to join the Order, in the teeth of a whole host of reasons to the contrary.

Admission to Religious Life

Father Gracián sets out these human reasons in his Autobiography, to which he gave the title *The pilgrim journey of Anastasio.*

I took the habit in Pastrana in 1572. I had struggled inwardly against this vocation for almost a year and a half and it was a decision that involved no small torment for me, because there were so many natural reasons that spoke against such a step. I am thinking first of the poor state of my health — whether due to a constitutional weakness or to exhaustion resulting from my studies — then of my obligations to my parents and siblings. For those who have positions at Court (and especially so my parents) have no other income or revenue but what is granted by the favour of the King, who pays their sons for their services if they show they are not unworthy of it. I had twelve siblings. One brother was private secretary to the King and he could have helped me acquire a profitable position in the Church so that I in turn could have helped the others. The King had already noticed me and asked me when I would obtain my doctorate, probably because he had an office in mind for me. In my studies I had become aware of some of the difficulties that there are in religious orders, and this meant that I was mentally far removed from having any thought of joining one of them.

Deep within me however all this conflicted with a burning desire to serve Our Lady, and Our Lady seemed to be turning my attention especially to the fact that reform had begun in her Order (the Carmelites). This thought often became so overpowering that I actually resorted on many occasions to putting a cover over a very beautiful image of the Holy Virgin that I possessed, as though this would block her call to me to take this service on myself. My confessors were no help, particularly the one in whom I had the greatest faith and to whom I offered the greatest obedience: he told me this was all quite clearly a temptation. I later heard from the mouth of Mother Teresa herself that it cost her a year of prayer to draw me into the Order after she had understood that I was the one who could help her...

The conflict left me in such a state that it was threatening my health and even my life, so great was my inner turmoil ...

Mother Teresa recounts from her side:

> Well then, while not having the slightest
> thought of taking the habit of this order, he was
> asked to go to Pastrana to speak to the prioress
> of our monastery there—for it had not yet been
> abandoned—that she might accept a nun. What
> means the Divine Majesty takes! For had Father
> Gracián decided to go there to take the habit
> himself, he would perhaps have met with so
> much opposition that he might never have done
> so. But the Blessed Virgin, Our Lady, to whom
> he is extremely devoted, wanted to repay him
> by giving him her habit. So I think she was the
> mediatrix through whom God granted him this
> favour. And this glorious Virgin was the reason
> he received it and became so fond of the order.
> She did not want one who desired to serve her
> so much to lack the occasion for putting this
> desire into practice. It is her custom to favour
> those who want to be protected by her…
>
> Well, the Virgin brought him to Pastrana as
> though by tricking him into the thought that he
> was going there in order to request the habit for
> a nun. And God brought him there in order to
> give him the habit. Oh, secrets of God! But how
> true that without our desiring it, He disposes
> us so as to give us favours.[1]

The saint is concerned to stress the indecisiveness,
indeed the complete innocence of Father Gracián:

> Well, when he arrived in Pastrana, he went to
> speak to the prioress that she might accept the
> nun; and it seemed as though he had asked her
> to pray to the Lord that he himself might enter.
> For he is a very pleasant person so that gener-
> ally he is loved by those who have dealings with

him—it is a grace our Lord gives—and thus he is extremely loved by all his subjects, both friars and nuns. Yet he doesn't let any fault go by, for he is extraordinarily careful in looking out for the welfare of the religious life. In his actions he is so gentle and pleasant that it seems no one is able to complain about him.

Well, when this prioress (Isabel de Santo Domingo) saw him, that which happened to others happened to her; she felt a strong desire that he enter the Order and told the Sisters how important it was to get him to join, for at the time there were very few, or almost none like him. And she told them all to beseech our Lord not to let him go without receiving the habit.

This prioress is a very great servant of God. By her prayer alone I think she would have been heard by His Majesty; how much more would the prayers of nuns as good as those that were there be heard. All of them took the matter very much to heart and with fasts, disciplines, and prayer begged His Majesty continually. Thus He was pleased to grant us this favour. For since Father Gracián went to the monastery of the friars and saw so much religious observance and opportunity to serve our Lord and above all that it was the order of the Lord's glorious Mother whom he so much desired to serve, his heart was moved not to return to the world...

Oh wisdom and power of God! How impossible for us to flee from His will! Our Lord truly saw the great need there was for a person like this to carry on the work that He had begun. I often praise Him for the favour He granted us in this matter. Had I very much desired to ask His Majesty for a person to organise all the things

pertaining to the order in these initial stages, I
would not have succeeded in asking for all that
He in fact gave in Father Gracián. May the Lord
be blessed for ever.[2]

While Teresa emphasised to her nuns the emotional
side of the spiritual life, God's wonderful guidance,
and the power of prayer—lived out in the midst of
their convent of nuns—Father Gracián laid the stress
on his inner struggle and firm deliberate choice. He
gave credit for his response to the Mother of God and
to Mother Teresa (ultimately almost indistinguisha-
ble!). Strangely, he did not say a single word about the
novice for whose sake he went to Pastrana, or about
the conversation with Teresa's Prioress:

> But in the end I could not endure the pressure
> of the thoughts arising from my love for Our
> Lady, and I said to myself: 'If there have been
> many noble men who were ready to lose pos-
> sessions, honour, and even life itself fighting
> duels for love of a worldly woman, how can I
> cling to anything when I am blinded by love for
> Our Divine Lady? If I am to die a few months
> after taking the habit because of the harshness
> of the life lived in the Order, I will count myself
> fortunate. For if the sheer harshness of life in
> this Order costs me my life, I am more than
> happy to lay it down for my Lady the Holy
> Virgin Mary. My resolve was so great, that
> when I then travelled to Pastrana, it was as
> though I was committing myself to a knightly
> career—such was the unshakableness of my
> resolve.

First difficulties

Gracián really did need to possess such firmness of resolve. Just at the moment when he entered, the priory came under the authority of a completely unsuitable Prior. His account of his life continues:

> The moment I entered the Order the difficulties began, for our Prior was called away by the Calced brothers to help them with the foundation of a priory in Madrid. He was giving instruction there to thirty novices who were later to be the flower of the Order. But we were so much left to our own devices that steps had to be taken to keep a few friars from acting imprudently, for they were ready to leave the Order on account of their Superior. All this gave us a great deal of work.

The unsuitable prior—Teresa later labelled him 'melancholy', an umbrella term she used to cover all possible psychological ailments—strove for an extreme penitential regime. In the absence of other friars possessed of a capacity for discrimination, life for a sensitive and cultured man was well-nigh unendurable in this environment:

> ... it happened that someone took a novice and was lashing his bare shoulders so that some damp wood would be set on fire by prayer alone, as our father Elijah had done. They thought that this was the way to know perfection. Other things of a similar type took place— the sort of ideas dreamed up by a kind of holy uncouthness that are liable to destroy the spirit and the creditworthiness of the Order, as St Jerome said.

> In the end everything was so horrific that I was thinking not to make my solemn profession but to leave the Order.
>
> … I imagined the time might come when I would be putting on the habit of the Calced.

Through the Prioress of Pastrana, Isabel de Santo Domingo, who had a shrewd understanding of what was needed to encourage Father Gracián, Mother Teresa had received news of his entry into the Order and of the difficulties he had been having within it. She talks quite candidly and openly about it in the Book of her Foundations (Ch. 23). But she also recognises here the positive aspect to the divine guidance, since the hard school of obedience that Father Gracián was going through helped him later on to be a good Superior.

> … God has given Father Fray Jerónimo de la Madre de Dios the greatest light in matters of obedience so that as one who had such a good initiation into its practice he might teach it to others. And that he might not lack experience … when the devil harassed him most to get him to give up the habit, he defended himself by promising to make his vows and not give it up.[3]

The difficulties in Pastrana did not arise solely from the ailing mind of a prior. A much bigger problem was that his state of mind and also the lack of education of a few of the friars had led to a fixation on a strange lady hermit who was beginning to be dangerous to Teresa's convents. Her name was Catalina de Cardona. This daughter of a Count had withdrawn to a cave near Alcalá and was revered as a saint. She acquired especial fame through the harshness of her penitential exercises. She lashed herself for hours with iron chains till the blood ran. The contrast with her earlier life heightened the impressiveness of it all, for quite apart from her noble origins she had lived as a courtly lady at the castle of Prince Eboli, to whom the town of Pastrana belonged. The Teresian monastery's interest in this strange holy woman grew excessive when Cardona, who always called herself simply 'the sinner', took the decision, on the basis of a vision, to found a convent of Discalced Carmelite Friars herself as well. To this end she entered into a brief correspondence with Teresa (who speaks of her with holy horror), and came to Pastrana to obtain everything necessary for the foundation (near her cave).

The eccentric hermit then had herself clothed as a monk. In her male habit she went off to Madrid, where she obtained the desired financial aid on the basis of her holy calling and with the help of her good connections at Court. She drove triumphantly in a carriage through the town accompanied by ladies singing hosannas. The frightful news then reached the ears of the papal Nuncio that a monk was sitting in a carriage surrounded by hordes of cheering women!

St Teresa, usually by preference very forthright, had no qualms about bluntly reporting the strange news about the rival founder of priories. But she also needed to take precautions, since she recognised the possibility of a split in the Order resulting from Pastrana. In order to avoid the development of any extreme tendencies, she needed a man who would know how to take the lead in Pastrana with mildness yet firmness. Father Gracián was a gift from heaven. But the commission which Teresa now resolved to give him filled him with fear. He must have felt doubly helpless, in that he had not yet even got to know the great reformer personally, though a few letters had been exchanged between them. He relates:

> What distressed me most that first year and was the beginning of many troubles that I had to endure, was that Mother Teresa of Jesus told the Discalced Carmelite nuns of Pastrana to obey me as if I were herself. Never before had she permitted any friar, whether calced or discalced, to take upon themselves any powers or authority of any kind, for she was fearful, as she confessed to me later tearfully, of the oppressive treatment habitually meted out by the friars to the nuns under the pretext of obedience, taking away from them the holy freedom of spirit to choose their own confessors, and depriving them of other things that gave them comfort: things that they treasured but which the friars despised.

> This trust that the Mother placed in me led her to transfer to a friar the obedience due to the bishops and it was a dangerous spark in the hearts of many, which later lit the great fire of which I shall speak. Then it aroused such a furious and consuming hatred in the souls of some of the friars that they began to slander some among the Discalced in the monastery of Pastrana and other monasteries ...

Teresa between Tact and Tactics

As Father Gracián quite rightly acknowledged, it was at this point that the real sufferings of his life started. Teresa herself was their first and last cause. Here began the persecutions in the Order, both from the Calced and from the Discalced, which later repeatedly threat-

ened to rob Jerónimo Gracián of what were humanly
speaking the highest values for him: honour and life!
For a Spaniard of his time these two were inseparable
concepts: honour had the same value as life, so dictated
Spanish law, and it was not only in the theatre that life
had to be sacrificed to honour.

But the threat that now hung over him had immeas-
urably deep roots, for it was actually connected with
the love of Saint Teresa. Indeed, something quite
astonishing was happening. The 57-year old Foundress, by her own testimony participator in the *Unio
mystica* and honoured for her life and her charism by
young and old, was giving her place to a green
novice—although not in respect of her office—we
should be clear about that—for Teresa was not Prioress
in Pastrana but in Avila. Her instructions that Father
Gracián was to be obeyed with the obedience due to
herself came out of the depths of her very being.

In Gracián's papers the following record was found:

> I do not know why the Mother leapt into
> making a concession quite unlike any that had
> ever been made to any friar. Priests ought
> generally only to preach and hear confessions,
> without possessing any further authority. This
> was quite clearly the root of all the subsequent
> difficulties and sufferings I went on to have in
> the Order not only in the Novitiate year but
> later—and not without justification, as I want
> to make crystal clear. The Mother was so holy
> and so very much loved by all her nuns, that
> each must have felt it as a painful thing that
> they were entrusted by her to a novice, espe-
> cially as she thereby passed over older and
> more worthy persons. They could not fail to
> notice the preferential treatment she increas-

ingly lavished on me. She must have been
mistaken on this point, and she thereby did me
a great deal of harm. When I reproached her for
it one day and told her off for loving me so
much and protecting me so openly, she just
laughed and said: 'My good father does not
know that each and every soul, however perfect
it may be, needs an outlet. Leave me this one
and say what you want: I have no intention of
changing my style of behaviour.'

Quite apart from any issues we cannot know about,
Teresa did have good reasons for what she did, reasons
that had to do with much wider issues than just the
particular situation in Pastrana. For this person who
was nothing less than an answer to prayer represented
to her a colleague and companion-in-arms for her in
all the affairs of the Order, or more precisely, for those
immense activities out of which the Order of 'Discalced
Carmelites' was to emerge. Teresa, 'a woman and
alone', as she so often stressed, was tired. Behind her
lay unbelievable struggles and battles as well as
disappointments, and she was now approaching her
sixtieth birthday. In four years she had founded seven
convents, and in addition there were the foundations
instituted by John of the Cross in Duruelo and Pastrana, for she was behind those too.

On top of all this, at the desire of her superior, the
Apostolic Visitor in Avila, Teresa took on the post of
Prioress in the Monastery of the Incarnation in 1571.
She did so reluctantly, for she had left this convent as
a prelude to the reform of the Order so as to found her
own small St Joseph's Convent. Now she had to go
back to the old one and reform it in the teeth of
considerable resistance. The task was so difficult that

Teresa began in a highly unusual way, which she must
have told Gracián about, for he recalled the following:

> When the first great meeting (the Chapter) was
> summoned and the nuns came into the assem-
> bly room inwardly hostile and very fearful, it
> was not Teresa who was sitting on the chair of
> the prioress: for she had placed a wonderfully
> beautiful picture of the Mother of God on the
> chair and sat at the feet of it. When the Sisters
> entered the room with their aggressive attitudes
> and then saw who had taken the place of the
> Prioress, many of them began to tremble all
> over, as they afterwards reported. They were
> so deeply moved that they felt ready for any
> service and prepared to accept any reform; this
> was what the humility and prayer of Mother
> Teresa had achieved through God, our Dear
> Lady, and St Joseph.

Teresa proceeded to give a most impressive address:

> My honoured Mother and Sisters! Obedience
> brings me to this house to serve you to your
> satisfaction as much as I am able. Each one of
> you can teach me and reform me. Therefore
> please think hard, my dear ladies, about what
> I can do for your cause. I will cheerfully see
> through everything that needs to be done, even
> if I have to give my blood and my life to do so.

The sisters were greatly impressed, but Teresa still had
to fight hard battles during this spell as Prioress, as for
example when she was personally obliged to throw
shameless visitors out of the House. Her sensitive heart
and her health were severely affected by all this, so
that in July 1573 she was writing to a friend who was
a Jesuit:

> May the grace of the Holy Spirit be with you. I
> wish I had more time for writing and better
> health; if I had, I would say a number of things
> which I think are important. But … I have been
> so incomparably worse than before that it will
> be as much as I can do to write what I am going
> to now; and I am such a tedious person that,
> however short I try to make the letter, it is sure
> to be a long one. This house of the Incarnation
> is evidently extremely bad for me. Please God
> I may win some merit here.[4]

Teresa was then overburdened and exhausted when
she put the young priest in her place. But in spite of all
the difficulties that grew out of this, her instinct was
fundamentally sound.

Father Gracián's three souls

This was the helper Teresa now needed, this highly
cultured man with his passion for the Order, his gentle
naturalness, and his carefree vitality; not to mention
his gifts as spiritual director, which would do honour
to any psychotherapist even in our day. His earthy
approach led him for example to counsel a depressive
nun to talk to her cat every day, and this helped her to
find her way out of her isolation to a better state of
health. His attitude towards 'supernatural' experiences
was rooted not in prejudices, but in a healthy scepticism, especially if these experiences involved a visual
dimension, which he completely rejected for himself.
His humour and his talent for anecdote enabled him
to take the edge from such things. Thus he reported
how the devil appeared to him one night at the age of
eleven—implying that it was probably a product of his
fear or fantasy—in the form of a billy-goat: '… shortly

before I came to a crossroads I began to feel absolutely terrified—so much so that my hair stood on end and lifted the velvet cap I was wearing right off my head …' But he bravely took a stone in each hand and went up against the big animal as if for a bullfight or a duel—then it disappeared. Later as a monk he spent the night with a fellow Carmelite in the house of the Cardinal of Toledo. Both of them saw in the garden there in front of the terrace railings, 'a huge ghost with a lot of arms, like an octopus, so scary that we took to our heels pronto. We ran so fast that Alberto, a lay brother we were taking with us, was astonished at the speed we were doing and concluded that we must have been in a race'.

It is typical of Gracián that a somewhat restrained kind of humour is evident in these accounts of visions, just as in his story of how the devil cried 'ay, ay, ay' bitterly at night, just because the papal Nuncio Sega had finally come down on the side of the good—i.e. the Teresian reform.

The question of visions was a burning one at that period, and that of sectarian contemplative movements was also to the fore. Both Teresa and Gracián were specialists in this area— Teresa through her practical experience, Gracián through his activity as father confessor and his great theoretical knowledge. Teresa, who at the beginning of her mystical 'career' had suffered a great deal under uncomprehending spiritual directors, was happy for her nuns to benefit from the guidance of this cautious man, whose humour and understanding were enriched by psychological empathy and self-awareness. This would become clear in a very delightful way after the death of Teresa, when he wrote his Dialogues, in which he divides his

personality between three persons and sketches out
their characters thus:

> At the time of evening recreation three friars
> had come together, looking for some recreation
> in pleasant conversation after the spiritual
> exertions of the day. One of them was called
> Anastasio[5], he had studied at a very young age
> at the University of Alcalá. He was a man with
> a lively mind and great intelligence. The soul
> of rationality, he was not willing to believe
> anything that had not been demonstrated by
> reason and science. The second was called
> Cirilo[6]. He was very well versed in out-of-the-
> way subjects and history. God had endowed
> him with an extremely powerful memory, and
> he had a profound knowledge of philosophy
> and classical languages. The third was called
> Eliseo[7]. He had a rather gentle nature and a
> pleasantly soft way of speaking, and he was a
> little credulous, especially when it was a ques-
> tion of unusual experiences like miracles, per-
> sonal revelations, and that kind of spiritual
> thing.

Gracián's writings show that he was to be preoccupied
with the status of visions all his life. For all that he
consistently emphasises that just the gospel and following Christ is enough, we still find him taking up
the question of inner contemplative experience again
and again. After all, Teresa herself confronts him with
it unavoidably, as will be seen. In his autobiographical
Dialogue, Anastasio trenchantly expresses Gracián's
own opinions but he is answered by Cirilo, the second
of Father Gracián's souls:

> You are all too insistent, Brother Anastasio,
> about rejecting these supernatural and extraor-

dinary spiritual things. Yet even if what you say
is all true and correct, that we should in fact fear
this extraordinary way of visions and revela-
tions rather than go after it, God is still
almighty; he can perform such miracles now
and at any time.

The last word went to Eliseo however, the third and
most gentle of Gracián's souls: 'Ultimately I am the
one who must take responsibility', said Eliseo, and if
I were to contribute anything, it would be to say that
I am quite fearful for you.'

Unwanted honours

Outwardly Father Gracián allowed more of a free rein
to the Anastasio-side of his soul, which was dominant
in his writings. His delicate sensitivities needed the
protection of reason, otherwise he could not indulge
his great passion, which in the language of the time
was called 'saving souls'. He shrank from no effort and
no sacrifice in the service of this passion and this
apostolate. Spiritual direction, the foundation of an
Order, everything served the one goal. He lived his
life in serene commitment.

So it was that the choice fell on him when it was a
question of straightening matters out in Seville. He
arrived there together with Father Mariano, one of the
founders of Pastrana, in August 1573, in order to bring
a 'wild' monastic foundation back into line. As a part
of this operation, he himself then founded a priory for
men (*Nuestra Señora de Los Remedios*), taking for its base
a wretched little hermitage. In doing so however, he
rather too generously overlooked the fact that the
General of the Order (Rossi—an Italian) had absolutely

prohibited the foundation of 'Discalced' priories for men in Andalusia.

Nonetheless Gracián was basically entitled to do this, since his Superior, the Apostolic Visitor, was authorised to override the authorities, as he sets out clearly in his Autobiography:

> We arrived, then, and asked Francisco de Vargas, Provincial of the Dominicans, who was at the time Apostolic Visitor of the Calced Carmelites of Andalusia by a Brief of Pius V, for a licence to carry out foundations. Not only did he give us this licence, he also entrusted to me the actual original Brief and installed me in his place as Apostolic Visitor. There I was now at twenty-eight years of age and a beginner as a friar, made Superior of the Calced Carmelites in Andalusia, inevitably in opposition to the General of all the Order, nor should it be forgotten that Andalusia was really the most ungovernable of all the Provinces. Just that on its own ought to suffice to give you some idea how I was likely to fare in this new office—a truly monstrous burden, given that the Province was riddled with jealousies and my own strength was so limited.

It was entirely understandable that the monks of the old Order, the so-called Calced, were hardly disposed to welcome having a young father of the Teresian Reform put in charge of them. They also quite correctly pointed out that although Gracián's Brief gave him the right to reform monasteries, it did not give him the right to found new ones. There were huge battles both out in the open and behind the scenes. In a letter of 14 May 1574 (the first extant letter of Teresa's in which the name of Gracián is mentioned) she made no bones about her delight:

> Oh, if you could see the to-do that is going
> on—secretly, of course—in favour of the Dis-
> calced! It is something one ought to praise the
> Lord for and it has all been aroused by the
> Fathers who went to Andalusia, Gracián and
> Mariano. My pleasure is greatly tempered by
> the distress it will cause our Father General, for
> whom I have such affection; on the other hand,
> I can see that our position was getting hopeless.
> You must all commend it to God.[8]

At the critical moment Pius V died, and with him the plenary powers granted by the Brief disappeared. Father Gracián saw himself completely abandoned. He needed the help of King Philip and the papal Nuncio and so he set off for Madrid. There he received more help than he had wished for. The King would have preferred to see the Jesuits as Visitators of contemplative orders, including the Carmelites, but the prudent Jesuits showed no interest. Consequently in June 1574 Gracián was appointed (at first provision-ally) by Nuncio Ormaneto as Provincial Vicar and Apostolic Visitor both of the Calced and of the Dis-calced Carmelites. Gracián sensed what was in store for him and would have preferred to refuse, but then the Discalced would have been deprived of his protec-tion. So initially he kept the appointment a secret and begged Mother Teresa for a meeting. At that point she was encountering problems with the foundation of a convent in Beas de Segura and needed Father Gracián with his authority on her side. They met in April. They must have had a very great deal to discuss, for they remained together for almost a month.

Notes

1 *Foundations* ch. 23, iv/vi/vii in *CW* iii, 218ff.
2 *Foundations* ch. 23, vii/viii/iii in *CW* iii, 219/20 & back to 218.
3 *Foundations* ch. 23, x in *CW* iii, 220.
4 *Letters* I, 119 no.46, 27 July 1573.
5 After Anastasios Sinaïtes, died c.700, an apostle to the heathen.
6 Cyril of Alexandria defended the status of Mary as Mother of God against the Nestorians at the Council of Ephesus in 431.
7 Elishah, prophet and successor to the legendary 'founder of the Order' Elijah.
8 *Letters* I, 135 no 53, to M. María Bautista, 14 May 1574.

3

THE BEST DAYS OF MY LIFE

A Fortunate Mistake

N THE YEAR 1567 Teresa had asked Rossi (in Spanish Rubeo), the General of her Order, for a Patent with full powers to found monasteries 'for the salvation of souls and to the glory of God'. Rubeo wrote:

> We cannot be unresponsive to this desire, which seems very Christian and holy to us. We must rather accept it, respond to it, and encourage it as much as we can. Therefore, in the exercise of our office as General of the Order, we empower the Reverend Carmelite Mother Teresa, at this time Prioress of the Convent of San José and subject in obedience to us, that she may accept or inherit houses, churches, and land anywhere in Castile as gifts for the purpose of founding convents for Carmelite nuns that are directly subjected to us. The nuns will wear a habit of brown sacking. If this is impossible to come by, coarse cloth may be used instead. Their life is to follow the original rule. Neither a Provincial nor a Vicar or Prior of this province is to exercise authority over them. That right is only for ourselves or for a commissary authorised by us. The number of nuns shall not exceed 25 in a convent.
>
> *Avila, 27 April 1567*

Unfortunately the expression 'Castile' was not quite clear, for as a kingdom it also included the Province of Andalusia. Therefore on 17 May the General sent a further appendix:

> We meant that our permission extends to Old and New Castile. This means that in the exercise of our office we give to the reverend Mother Teresa rights and authority to accept, acquire, erect, and found convents of nuns anywhere in the kingdom of Castile but not however in Andalusia.

Two years later the General confirmed the trust and respect to which these powers testified in a very personal way. In a letter addressed to the nuns of the newly-founded monastery in Medina del Campo, a letter which Teresa—who was present there too at the time—would also read, he wrote:

> I would like to give infinite thanks to His divine Majesty for so many favours granted to our Order through the wisdom and endeavour of our reverend Teresa de Jesus. This reverend mother brings more profit to the Order than all of our Carmelite Friars in Spain together. May God give her many years of life! I admonish you all, my reverend sisters, to obey the aforesaid Teresa in everything, she is your true Superior and you must know what a precious jewel you possess in this wonderful friend of God.

Teresa always followed the directives of the highest authority with the greatest care. When she made a foundation in Beas at the beginning of the year 1575 she had concluded that her monastery stood on Castilian territory. However there was an element of uncertainty: in April she received a grant of powers couched in Latin, which again only generally said *'quot constituere posset omnibusque locis'* —that she was allowed to make foundations everywhere. So in acknowledging her mistake to the General on 18 May, she did not really apologise, but said:

> Your Reverence must also know that I made enquiries everywhere before coming to Beas, so as to be sure it was not Andalusia, where I had not the least intention of making a foundation, as I do not care for the people. It turns out that Beas is not Andalusia, but is a Province of Andalusia.[1]

By 'province' Teresa meant the ecclesiastical province. Father Gracián gave a clear explanation of this later:

> Research revealed that in terms of secular jurisdiction Beas belonged to the Castilian administration, but in ecclesiastical jurisdiction to Andalusia. That raised problems for myself and for Mother Teresa, for to tell the truth she possessed authority neither from the General of the Order nor from the Visitor to make foundations in Andalusia. Therefore the foundation completed in February was not good, and if Mother Teresa had known the position, she would on no account have gone to Beas and founded the convent.

Teresa herself relates the prehistory to all this:

> When I was sent, as mentioned, from the Incarnation to Salamanca, a messenger came there from the town of Beas with letters for me from a lady in that area and from the curate beneficiary there. The letters contained both the offer of a benefice from that town and requests from other persons asking me to come and found a

monastery. They already had a house; all that
was needed was to go and make the foundation.

When questioned by me, the man recounted
wonderful things about the land, and rightly
so, for it is very delightful and has a good
climate. But in considering the distance, many
leagues from here, the notion of making a
foundation there seemed to me foolish. Especially so, since I was under the orders of the
apostolic commissary (Fernandez OP), who, as
I mentioned, was opposed to, or at least not in
favour of, my making foundations. So I wanted
to answer that I was unable, and avoid asking
permission of the apostolic commissary about
it. Afterward, it seemed to me that since he was
present at that time in Salamanca and I had
received the order from our Reverend Father
General not to fail to make foundations, it
would be unwise to refuse without getting his
opinion.[2]

The saint went on to relate how the Dominican Visitator Pedro Fernández became an instrument of God's
and Teresa's purposes against his own intentions.
While praising the pious intention of the foundress, he
pointed out that ecclesiastically Beas was subject to the
Order of the Knights of St James and that permission
must be given by them—and in Teresa's view he
clearly anticipated that such permission would be
refused. Very surprisingly however, the Knightly
Order actually approved the foundation. Fernández
had been hoist by his own petard and so had to agree,
and the foundation took place on 24 February. Obviously this spiritual Superior was far from well-in-
formed himself about the geographical-juridical
boundaries. It all came out only after the monastery

had been consecrated and occupied. Extremely worried, Teresa made a plan to travel to Beas. She wrote to Rubeo:

> ... I did not learn this till over a month after the foundation had been made. By that time I was already there with the nuns, and I felt that I ought not to abandon the foundation. That was one reason why I came here ...[3]

One of the reasons .... But there was also Father Gracián with his troubles: Father Gracián who had founded a monastery of Discalced Carmelites in Seville without the permission of Rubeo, and whose supplications had led King and Nuncio all too enthusiastically and all too eagerly to hand him powers for Andalusia—against the will of the General of the Order. In vain had Gracián resisted, in vain his brother warned the King. Father Jerónimo wrote later:

> It was difficult, after only a year in the Order to find the requisite humility and self-denial to take on a difficult charge like this of reforming the Calced Carmelites, where discontentment and malicious gossip would be snapping at my heels. But when I exchanged letters on the question with Mother Teresa, she and her friends made me aware that they really felt I should take up this cross. Otherwise there was a great danger that the Calced would work for the downfall of the monasteries of the 'Discalced'. They thought that as Superior of all the Calced and Discalced of Andalusia I could with one hand encourage the development of the Discalced monasteries while with the other I was protecting them against the attacks of the Calced. It would be far better if the latter had me in their sights rather than the Discalced. In

order to be able to discuss all this more fully, I
agreed by letter with the Mother that we should
meet in the newly-founded convent at Beas. She
informed me of her arrival and I came to Beas
to see the one whom I had been ardently
longing to know, for up to then we had been in
touch only by letter.

The encounter in Beas

Teresa's version of events is as follows:

> When ... the Father Maestro Fray Jerónimo
> Grácian came to see me at Beas, we had never
> previously met although I had very much
> desired to meet him. (Yes, at times, we had
> corresponded.) I was extremely delighted when
> I learned he was there, for I greatly desired to
> meet him on account of the good reports given
> me concerning him. But much greater was my
> happiness when I began speaking with him, for
> it seemed from the way he pleased me that
> those who had praised him had hardly known
> him at all.
>
> Since at that time I had so many difficulties, it
> seems that when I saw him the Lord showed
> me the good that was going to come to us
> through him. So during those days I went about
> with such excessive consolation and happiness
> that indeed I was surprised at myself. At that
> time he did not have authority outside Andalu-
> sia. It was when he was in Beas that the Nuncio
> sent to see him and then gave him authority
> over the discalced friars and nuns of Castile. So
> much joy did my spirit feel that I couldn't thank
> our Lord enough these days, nor did I want to
> do anything else.[4]

Here Teresa brings together events which in her mind meld seamlessly into one another. It was in fact literally the case that Gracián came around the middle of April to Beas and then went to Madrid shortly before 12 May. There his appointment for Andalusia of 8 and 13 June 1574 was not only confirmed but on 3 August extended to the Discalced of Castile. He was now Provincial Vicar, Apostolic Visitator, and Reformer for the Calced and Discalced friars and nuns of Andalusia as well as being Apostolic Visitator for the Discalced monks and nuns of Castile.

The double delight that Teresa speaks of was thus connected to what happened in the months of May and August. She returned to this subject a second time to outline the significance she attributed to Gracián in the history of the Order:

> Although he was not the one who first began, he came along at the right moment. For sometimes I would have regretted ever having begun had it not been for the great confidence I had in the mercy of God.

Teresa added that she was thinking above all of the conditions in the men's priories of Andalusia prior to when 'Our Lord provided a remedy through the Father Maestro Fray Jerónimo de la Madre de Dios.'[5]

Gracián has left his own account of what the first encounter meant to him:

> I stayed a long time in Beas, and we ended up discussing all the affairs of the Order, past, present, and future, for which provision had to be made. We also spoke about the spirit of the Order and how we could bring it to the monks and the nuns and how they could remain in it. The Mother asked me what I knew theoretically

and practically in this matter, and taught me everything she knew herself, so that I could write a thick book about all the teaching, instructions, and counsels that I received from her. Many days elapsed and we spent all the time—only excepting mealtimes and holy Mass—in these conversations.

She gave me an account of her life, her spiritual experiences, and her aims, and I became so devoted to her that from then on I would not undertake any important project without asking for her advice. She herself had a problem at that point, which we talked about for a long time, for she had no licence for foundations in Andalusia, and the General was annoyed with me over my foundation in Seville. For my part I could not go to Castile, since I was commissioned only for Andalusia. So together we lamented the fact that while we were united in our hearts we were separated by our roles.

However, with the help of the Franciscans Gracián did some research into the status of the town of Beas, and was delighted to discover that canonically it belonged to Andalusia. He showed Teresa all the papers he had found which established him as her Superior in Andalusia and allowed him the pleasure of acting as a *Deus ex machina*.

I commissioned her all over again to found the (already founded) convent in Beas and began to behave towards her as Superior and father confessor; she was far from unhappy about it, for the mistake that had been uncovered opened the way for her to make further foundations in Andalusia, and she recognised the great help of God in all this.

Teresa too writes of their exceptional affection and inner agreement:

> It will seem inappropriate that he should have informed me of so many personal matters about his soul. Perhaps the Lord wanted this that I might record it here, and He might be praised in His creatures. For I know that neither to any confessor nor to any other person has this Father manifested so much about himself. At times he had reason for so doing because he thought that on account of my age and from what he heard about me I had some experience. It was while we were speaking about other matters that he told me about these things and additional ones that cannot be suitably put in writing, for I would be going on at much greater length.
>
> Certainly, I have used much restraint so that if this work should ever get into his hands he won't suffer pain. I couldn't help it, nor did it seem to me (for if this work is to be seen, it won't be for a long time yet) that one who did so much good for the renewal of the observance of the primitive rule should be forgotten.[6]

Both Teresa and the young priest were deeply affected by their meeting. Suffering from an intense loneliness (at least inwardly), Gracián opened up his whole heart to her. It must surely have been Teresa's motherliness that touched him most of all—her 'years' and her 'experience' (as she herself recognised very perceptively). The 'experience' in question refers to the sphere of God's love that bound the two of them together in a timeless relationship.

Subsequent remarks made by Father Gracián reveal
how deeply his heart was touched by the charm of the
saint and by her unique femininity, something that
found expression not just in her soul but in her body
too. His 'beautiful Teresa' (see Chapter 1) reappears in
remarks like: 'She had very graceful features that
moved one to surrender to her inwardly.' Four years
later, he rather sadly registered a change in her, and
in doing so proved that he had known in Teresa not
only the Mother, but also the attractive woman:

> In 1579, in the year of the great influenza
> epidemic, Mother Teresa was staying in Val-
> ladolid. She was so seriously ill there that she
> had well nigh gone to her eternal blessedness.
> After this illness she was so changed and had
> lost so much weight that for the first time her
> age began to show. Until then her personality
> and the beauty of her looks had outshone her
> constant illnesses to such an extent that she had
> looked much younger than she was.

While Father Gracián saw in Teresa both beauty and
youthfulness, what struck Teresa most forcefully about
him was the maturity he had in spite of his youth.
Convinced earlier than anyone else that her Reformed
Order needed an independent status, she wrote to
King Philip II:

> It would be an extremely good thing if, at this
> early stage (in the life of the Reform), it were
> put in charge of a Discalced Father named
> Gracián, with whom I have recently become
> acquainted. Though young, he has given me
> great cause to praise Our Lord for the spiritual
> gifts He has bestowed on him, and the great
> works He has wrought through him, which

have helped many of the nuns, so I think the Lord has chosen him for the great good of this Order.[7]

Youth is attracted to maturity, maturity to youth. But the deep personal impact they had on each other was intimately connected with their shared love for God and with the apostolate they were fulfilling in the service of the Order and of their fellows.

Gracián became increasingly more absorbed than Teresa in the work involved in his particular vocation. Her feminine sensitivities, as well as the limitless capacity for love she derived from the *Unio mystica*, consistently led her to give the priority to the human side over all the constraints imposed by facts. Later this was to cause conflict, but those first weeks they spent together in Beas and those that followed filled the saint with unmitigated joy. While Father Gracián, chivalrous man that he was, adopted an attitude of the greatest reserve, Teresa sent letters to the four corners of the earth telling of her newfound happiness:

> O, Mother, how much I have wished you were with me during these last few days! I must tell you that, without exaggeration, I think they have been the best days of my life. For over three weeks we have had Father-Master Gracián here; and, much as I have had to do with him, I assure you I have not yet fully realized his worth. To me, he is perfect, and better for our needs than anyone else we could have asked God to send us. What your Reverence and all the nuns must do now is to beg His Majesty to give him to us as a superior. If that happens, I can take a rest from governing these houses, for anyone so perfect, and yet so gentle, I have never seen. May God have him in His

keeping, and preserve him; I would not have missed seeing him and having to do with him for anything in the world.

He has been waiting here for Mariano, who, to our great delight, took a long time to arrive. Julián de Ávila is lost in admiration for him and so are all the rest. He preaches marvellously. I feel sure he must have improved a great deal since you saw him.

Obviously Prioress Inés had also got to know Father Gracián, but without however wholly sharing Teresa's enthusiasm. Teresa wrote in the same letter: 'I feel sure he must have improved a great deal since you saw him: the severe trials he has suffered will have done him a lot of good.'[8]

Like an angel

Now the sky was blue over Andalusia. Teresa wrote to her sister Juana de Ahumada to tell her that as Apostolic Commissary and Visitator, Gracián had received authority over all the Discalced of Castile and of Andalusia, 'nothing better could have happened to us'.[9] However, before Gracián could exert his full authority, the ruffled feathers of the General of the Order needed to be smoothed. Teresa brought to bear all her womanly charms and all her diplomatic skills in her role as mediator. She repaid Rubeo his former compliment of Medina del Campo: ' ... I beg your Reverence to realize that the whole body of the Discalced Fathers means nothing to me by comparison with anything that so much as touches your Reverence's garment.'[10]

She then made a point of saying that Gracián was not present (so she was writing on her own initiative) and stressed his innocence, for he had his authority from the Visitator, behind whom stood the Pope. (This of course is always the heaviest artillery in any battle over jurisdiction.) In a nutshell, she concluded, 'Gracián is like an angel!'.

Evidently the General did not pay too much heed to such angels, for the end of January 1576 found the saint writing to him once again about the same business. The letter counts as one of the most celebrated in world literature. Teresa stated emphatically that Gracián himself would rather have refused an office that was as difficult as it was elevated: but in the interests of the Order and in the name of God he eventually concluded that he had to take it on. Calling on divine support, she then became quite forceful:

> ... I hope in God that, if your reverence [i.e. the General] will show this Father favour so that he may know he is in your good graces, everything will work out quite well.

> ... If there were a great many men to whom this task could be entrusted (it would be another matter) but, as there seem to be none with the gifts which this Father has—and I am quite sure, if you saw him, you would agree ...[11]

This letter was very far from being a mere exercise in charm, for Teresa was staking all on winning the General over. It was no occasion for the utterance of mere formulae of humility:

> But let your Reverence remember that children are apt to err, and that fathers must not look at their faults, but forgive them. For the love of Our Lord, I beseech your Reverence to do me this favour. Bear in mind that it would be

advisable for many reasons which perhaps, being so far away, you do not understand as well as I do here, and that, although we women are not of much use as counsellors, we are occasionally right...

When we both stand before His judgement seat, your Reverence will see what you owe to your loyal daughter, Teresa of Jesus.[12]

She wrote in quite intimate terms to her friend and cousin María Bautista, Prioress in Valladolid, though the letter also provides evidence of certain tensions which there had been with this lady — and not for the last time. The serenity of Teresa's justification was balanced by a tone of unrestrained jubilation that she had found this man who gave fulfilment to her heart:

As concerns ... my friendship with him, you would be amazed at what is happening. I have been unable to do otherwise, and I am not at all repentant. If your Reverence finds faults in him, it will be because you seldom see him or have anything to do with him. I assure you he is a saintly man, and not in the least headstrong, but very cautious. I know this from experience and it would be safe to trust him with more (precious things) than (these) books. You say if I feel like that about him I must be forgetting my Father Fray Damián (Domingo Bañez). The reason will be that the one is so different from the other ... friendship that involves attachment to nothing but things of the spirit. It is like having to do with an angel, for that is what he is and has always been. At the same time, the other person I have mentioned is an angel too, and I do not know why I have been tempted (to think more of the one than of the other), for it

is quite a different thing. Blessed be God, he is
better. Give him my remembrances.[13]

The lines that follow in this letter are blurred (and in
addition it survives only in mutilated form), and I
would not risk attempting a translation of the unclear
passages. We can be certain only of Teresa's anxiety
that Father Gracián might lose his '*libertad santa*', his
'holy liberty' through this love, an anxiety which she
now realised had been unnecessary. This she felt also
applied to herself: 'that other friendship, as I say,
rather gives freedom. That is a quite different thing
...'[14]

Far from hindering her from living for God, this
friendship actually freed her for it. The sentence: 'he
is an angel and always was' recalls what Teresa later
wrote to King Philip about John of the Cross: ' ...
people look on him as a saint, which, in my opinion,
he is and has been all his life.'[15]

This last shrewd assessment of Teresa's is often
cited. Why then do people not trust her judgement
over Father Gracián? Even in a modern and progres-
sive Spanish biography it is still stated that Teresa, at
the high point of her life and familiar with the condition of *Unio mystica* 'allowed herself to be blinded' by
the young father. To say nothing of other judgements
that have been passed on her. The letter above shows
how right from the beginning Teresa saw very clearly
that such misinterpretations would be possible. Did
her expression 'angel' frighten posterity? Does it point
to womanly raptures? Is an angel more than a saint—
because superhuman—or less because he can fall such
a frightful distance? Does this expression 'give wings'
to the fantasy of posterity? What Teresa actually
wanted to stress by using the term was the innocent

purity of this young man and of their mutual love. That is why she spoke of freedom. For she recognised 'the precious and longed-for freedom of the spirit' as the 'sign of perfection'.

At the end of the letter cited she writes in combative excitement: 'Give him my very kind regards. I assure you it is a great effort to me not to write to him. Do not be afraid that anyone will take away this friendship, which has cost a great deal.'[16] This is not a siren voice, it is the sound of a fanfare!

Clearly there was still some defending to do. Three months later she wrote to the same Prioress again but more calmly:

> It is a strange thing that my affection for this other Father of ours no more embarrasses me than if there were no such person. I fancy he does not know that I am writing to you now. He is very well ... If I had been allowed to leave here, I should have been with you by this time ... For many reasons which cannot be put into a letter your convent is the one I should like to choose: one of them is that I should be near my Father and near you.'[17]

Not all nuns may do this

Such letters may have aroused a certain amount of excitement in the Order. But what did Teresa write to Father Gracián himself? The first surviving letter dates from 27 September 1575, hence four months after the happy weeks in Beas. The subjects discussed, the familiar tone, and especially the coded names each use such as 'Laurencia' and 'Eliseo' force us to the conclusion that here we have only a part of a much longer correspondence. The somewhat insecure postal service of the time always left open the possibility that a letter would be read by someone other than the one for whom it was intended. Hence Teresa introduced meaningful and often witty pseudonyms: for important personalities, for the two separating branches of the Order, even for Jesus Christ, when she reports on her inner experience, and not least for the Father Gracián and for herself. Often she calls herself Laurencia, an allusion to her favourite brother Lorenzo,[18] but more often Angela.

Teresa was very far from regarding herself as an 'angel'—unless she had some notion of using the word to express the purity of her own love, in the same way that she used it for Father Gracián when she called him 'angel'—so Gracián may have been the one who pitched on this name for her. I have discovered no definite evidence of this, yet it is striking how frequently the name of St Angela of Foligno crops up in his extensive works—and often without any obvious reason. St Angela was told in a vision by Christ that love for God united with love for neighbour were the true signs of the *Unio mystica* and quite beyond the reach of the devil. In Teresa's *Soliloquies* it says:

> Oh, my Jesus, how great is the love You bear the children of men, for the greatest service one can render You is to leave You for their sake and their benefit—and then You are possessed more completely … while we live this mortal life, earthly joys are uncertain, even when they seem to be given by You, if they are not accompanied by love of neighbour. Whoever fails to love his neighbour, fails to love You, my Lord, since we see You showed the very great love You have for the children of Adam by shedding so much blood.[19]

Wherever it was that Teresa found her pseudonym 'Angela'—which eventually became the only name that Father Gracián used for her—the important thing is what the sentences cited above tell us about the conception the two shared of their Christian task and about their own human togetherness.

The pseudonyms which Teresa gave Father Gracián in her letters are all connected with his activity and calling in the Order. At first she calls him Eliseo (Elishah), seeing him as the successor to the Prophet Elijah of Mount Carmel, to whom the reformed Order looked as its father. But her choice of this pseudonym was also in part dictated by her tender-playful view of the priest: despite his youth, Gracián was bald-headed. Loving as she was, Teresa felt sorry for him with regard to this 'failing' and wanted to pour balm on what could have been a sore point.

In the Second Book of Kings it is said of Elishah: ' … while he was on the road, some small boys came out of the town and jeered at him. 'Hurry up, baldy', they shouted. 'Come on up, baldy!''.[20] The most important element in the pseudonym however was Gracián's role as successor to Elijah:

> … the two of them stood by the Jordan. Elijah took his cloak, rolled it up and struck the water; and the water divided to left and right, and the two of them crossed over dry shod. When they had crossed, Elijah said to Elishah, 'Make your request. What can I do for you before I am snatched away from you?' Elishah answered, 'Let me inherit a double share of your spirit.' 'Your request is difficult', Elijah said. 'If you see me while I am being snatched away from you, it will be as you ask: if not, it will not be so.' Now as they walked on, talking as they went,

a chariot of fire appeared and horses of fire coming between the two of them; and Elijah went up to heaven in the whirlwind. Elishah saw it and shouted, 'My father! My father! Chariot of Israel and its chargers!' Then he lost sight of him, and taking hold of his own clothes he tore them in half. He picked up Elijah's cloak which had fallen, and went back and stood on the bank of the Jordan. He took Elijah's cloak and struck the water. 'Where is Yahweh, the God of Elijah?' he cried. As he struck the water it divided to right and left, and Elishah crossed over. The brotherhood of prophets saw him in the distance and said, 'The spirit of Elijah has come to rest on Elishah'; they went to meet him and bowed to the ground before him.[21]

The use of the name 'Paul' for Gracián first began a year later, in September 1576. Teresa associates Gracián with the immense zeal of the Apostle to the Gentiles, his powerful sermons, his culture, his persecutions, and his sufferings. And at the deepest level: Christ in him. 'Cyrillus', the name of the great defender of the divine motherhood of Mary, occurs in a letter of 19 November 1576, when the question was raised as to whether Visitators ought also to approve the foundation of women's convents, for which Teresa sought the agreement of Father Gracián. He himself preferred to use the name 'Cyrillus' in his later writings, even if as a secondary figure. By contrast we find him using the name 'Anastasio', the apostle to the heretics, in place of the name 'Paul' (which Teresa greatly preferred). 'Eliseo' (Elishah) was used by her in the surviving letters only nine times, perhaps so as not to give too many reminders of his baldness. For the first time on 27 September 1575:

'As the visitation there has already been made, I have
been wondering if he (P. Baltasar de Jesús) wants to
go to his lair in order to avoid meeting my Eliseus.'[22]

The depth of feeling evident in just the word 'my'
alone is unmistakable. At the end of the letter 'Laurencia' utters tender complaints that the Lord is testing
her, for he has given her a father confessor who is sadly
so taken up with problems 'that she will enjoy very
little of his company.'[23]

In this same letter we also encounter quite uncon-
cealed expressions of her deeply spiritual love for
Gracián, a love that Teresa expresses by the word
caridad (Lat. *caritas*):

> I realize what charity (*caridad*) your Paternity
> has shown me—not only great in itself, but all
> the greater because it has been done in such a
> way as to leave me without scruples. And now
> I think it is my turn to show I have a little
> charity; for, deeply as I feel your Paternity's
> absence, I should be glad for you to stay away
> for another month, on condition that you would
> do something to help the Incarnation and they
> gave you charge of that house. Even a week
> would be long enough if you could leave Fray
> John (of the Cross) there as vicar.[24]

With all due respect to John of the Cross, it was her
soulmate Eliseo that Teresa preferred to have with her.
Gracián for his part was often worried by her open
pronouncements of love and enthusiasm, but by now
Teresa had become quite sure of herself, and she began
to use the word *amor* too and confessed it openly. This
was not however a matter of someone getting inno-
cently involved in something dangerous. Already in
The Way of Perfection (1562-1565) we find in Chapter 6:

Let us return now to the love that it is good for
us to have, that which I say is purely spiritual.
I don't know what I am saying. At least I don't
think it's necessary to speak much about this
love, because few have it. Let the one to whom
the Lord has given it praise Him very much
because such a person may have reached the
highest perfection.[25]

Teresa's acknowledgement that she has this maturity
does not indicate some departure from her customary
humility. In her way of thinking, humility is connected
to a recognition of the dignity which God has granted
to the soul and which cannot be squared with any
constraint or bondage, as she explains in the first
'Dwelling' of the *Interior Castle*. Self-knowledge, she
adds, is indeed essential in the highest stage of development, yet it is just as important that we raise
ourselves more and more to the contemplation of the
greatness of God, who works in the inmost core of the
soul.

A sign of the enduring depth of her union with God
is to be found in a quite crucial letter in which Teresa
both warns Father Gracián against an excessive openness and carefreeness while at the same time also
imperiously confessing her love. She writes:

With time you will lose some of that simplicity
you have, which I am sure is the virtue of a
saint. But, as the devil is unwilling that everyone should be a saint, those who, like myself,
are wicked and malicious are anxious to
deprive him of his opportunities. For many
reasons it is permissible for me to feel great
affection for you and to show it in the dealings
we have together. But it is not permissible for
all the other nuns to do so. Nor are all superiors

like my Father, who allows people to treat him
with such frankness.

… And when the sisters observe that I say and
do things which are allowable in me because of
my age and because I know whom I am dealing
with they will quite naturally think they can do
the same. In saying this I am not loving them
any the less: I am acting out of the very strongest affection for them.

I can say truly that, wicked though I am, I have
been so restrained and circumspect where my
daughters are concerned, ever since I first had
any, and I have had so sharp an eye on ways in
which the devil could tempt them through me,
that—glory be to God, for His Majesty has been
gracious to me in this—I believe there are few
of my very serious faults that they are able to
see. I confess too, I have tried to conceal my
imperfections from them, though these are so
numerous that they must have seen a great
many of them, as well as my love for Paul and
the concern I have for his welfare. I often
represent his importance to the Order and the
(consequent) necessity (for my acting as I do);
were he not here to help me, I should give up
entirely.

But how wearisome I am getting! Yet my Father
must not be wearied by listening to what I say,
for your Paternity and I bear the load of a very
heavy burden, and we shall have to render an
account to God and the world. Realizing, as you
do, with what love I am addressing you, you
will be able to forgive me, and to do me the
kindness, as I have begged you, of not reading
in public the letters I write you. Remember
there are many different types of mind and

> there are some things which superiors should
> not speak about too openly. There may be
> things like that which I write about myself or
> about a third person, and which it would be
> better that nobody should know. There is a
> great difference between the way I treat your
> Paternity privately and the way I talk of you to
> other people, even to my own sisters. Just as I
> should not like anyone to overhear my conver-
> sations with God or to disturb me when I am
> alone with Him, so it is with Paul …[26]

Teresa knew that there was something much more
fundamental at stake here than the natural attraction
of a woman to her charming and understanding father
confessor, who could be a help or a hindrance to her
on her way. Teresa's love streamed out of the *Unio
mystica*, it was kept in equilibrium by God's love which
had chosen the young Father Gracián. God's love is
fiery and deeply disturbing, we can see that both by
looking at Christ and by mystical experience. But this
stream of love out of the heart of the soul, out of the
innermost core of the being, is protected from becoming a prison of egoistic desire. Gracián himself was all
too aware of that. He declared later in the 'Pilgrimage
of Anastasio' to Cirilo, his conversation partner repre-
senting another part of his soul:

> … and for you to understand this properly, you
> must know that Mother Teresa loved me most
> tenderly and I loved her more than any other
> creature on earth … But this very great love that
> I had for Mother Teresa and she for me is of a
> very different character from the love that we
> are used to in this world, which causes danger
> and confusion. It gives rise to thoughts and
> temptations that are not good, for they distress

the spirit and sap its energies and stir up sensuality. But this love I bore to Mother Teresa and she to me gave me purity, spiritual graces, and love of God, and to her it gave consolation and relief in all her labour, sufferings, and troubles, as she told me many times: for that reason she wanted her love for me to surpass even my own mother's. Blessed be God who sent me such a great friend; now that she lives in heaven, her love is warm and alive and I am sure that it will be very beneficial for my life. But you are also familiar with the type of twisted mentality that will persist in drawing from our great closeness and mutual trust the conclusion that this could not possibly be a holy love. In reality however the truth is that even if she not had been as holy as she was, and I had been the most evil man in the world, the fact that she was a woman of sixty who lived such a withdrawn and honourable life ought to have been sufficient to free her from any taint of evil suspicion. Nonetheless it was better for us to keep a low profile with our intimate friendship for the sake of not causing a scandal.

This inner friendship had its sole basis in the visions that were vouchsafed to Teresa after their first meeting. It was these that determined the character of their subsequent personal relationship.

Notes

1   *Letters* I, 179 no 74, 18 June 1575.
2   *Foundations* ch. 22, i, ii in *CW* iii, 207.
3   *Letters* I, 179 no 74, 18 June 1575.
4   *Foundations* ch. 24, i, ii in *CW* iii, 222.
5   *Foundations* ch. 23, xii in *CW* iii, 221.
6   *Foundations* ch. 23, xi/xii in *CW* iii, 221.

7   *Letters* I, 188 no 77, 19 July 1575.
8   *Letters* I, 175 no 72, 12 May 1575.
9   *Letters* I, 190 no 78, 12 Aug 1575.
10 *Letters* I, 180 no 74, 18 June 1575.
11 *Letters* I, 222/223 no 91, Feb 1576.
12 *Letters* I, 223/221 no 91, Feb 1576.
13 *Letters* I, 194 no 78a, 28 Aug 1575.
14 *Letters* I, 195 no 78a, 28 Aug 1575.
15 *Letters* I, 496 no 204, 4 Dec 1577.
16 *Letters* I, 195 no 78a, 28 Aug 1575.
17 *Letters* I, 211 no 87, 30 Dec 1575.
18 Perhaps also, according to her editor P. Silverio OCD, a reference to St Laurence, the fire of whose death was regarded as symbolic of the fire of love.
19 *Soliloquies* ii in *CW* i, 376.
20 1 K 2, 23.
21 2 K 2, 7-15.
22 *Letters* I, 197 no 79, 27 Sept 1575.
23 *Letters* I, 199 no 79, 27 Sept 1575.
24 *Letters* I, 198 no 79, 27 Sept 1575.
25 *Way of Perfection* ch. 6 in *CW* ii, 62.
26 *Letters* I, 345 no 134, Nov 1576.

4

THE CONTRACT

Vision and truth

O F ALL TERESA'S visions in which Gracián appeared, the first was the most important and life-changing. The account of it runs like this:

> In 1575, during the month of April, while I was at the foundation in Beas, it happened that the Master Friar Jerome Gratian of the Mother of God came there. I had gone to confession to him at times, but I hadn't held him in the place I had other confessors, by letting myself be completely guided by him. One day while I was eating, without any interior recollection, my soul began to be suspended and recollected in such a way that I thought some rapture was trying to come upon me; and a vision appeared with the usual quickness, like a flash of lightning.

> It seemed to me our Lord Jesus Christ was next to me in the form in which He usually appears, and at His right side stood Master Gratian himself, and I at his left. The Lord took our right hands and joined them and told me He desired that I take this master to represent Him as long as I live, and that we both agree in everything because it was thus fitting.

> I remained with very great assurance that the vision was from God. The remembrance of the two confessors I had gone to and followed for a

long time and to whom I owed a great deal made
me undecided. The remembrance of one especially (Fr Domingo Bañez OP) made me put up
strong resistance, ... for I had great respect and
love for him. In spite of this I felt assurance from
the vision that such an action suited me, and also
comfort from the thought that the consultations
with persons of different opinions was now at
an end. For some, by not understanding me,
made me suffer very much; although I never
gave up any of them until either they moved
away or I did, because I thought the fault was
mine. Twice more the Lord returned to tell me
in different words not to fear since He gave
Master Gratian to me. So I resolved not to do
otherwise, and I made the proposal within
myself to carry out the Lord's request for the rest
of my life ...

I was left with a peace and comfort so great I
was amazed, and I felt certain the Lord wanted
this, for it doesn't seem to me the devil could
give me such great peace and comfort of soul...
I again praise our Lord and remember that
verse which says, '*Qui posuit fines suos in pace*',[1]
and I want to be consumed in the praises of
God.[2]

The struggle over this full subjection had been hard.
Teresa says:

I don't think I did anything in my life over
which I felt within myself greater resistance —
not even when I made my profession — except
when I left my father's house ...[3]

We might speculate perhaps that at this point Teresa
was catching up on something that is so often a part
of a woman's destiny: complete consecration and

abandonment of person and life to a beloved man. We might of course ask why Christ 'was not enough' for this. It is certain that Teresa was well aware of the problem.

After much inner struggle she recognises that her personal promise of obedience is to be made only in the Holy Spirit. Consequently the Holy Spirit in turn is obliged 'to give the light with which he enlightens me' to Father Gracián too. She now promises trustfully to hide nothing from him, to obey him for the rest of her life in all important matters, 'in short, to take him inwardly and outwardly in place of God'. That sounds shocking initially. But we must take very careful note of Teresa's commentary. Of Father Gracián she says: 'Praised be the Lord, that he created a man who is completely filled by Him.'

Teresa makes her promise 'in order to do this service to the Holy Spirit'. Afterwards she not only experiences joy, relief, and a wonderful peace, but also acquires a whole new freedom: '… And so I remained with great satisfaction and happiness, and I have remained so since then. And although I feared I might be restricted, I was left with greater freedom'[4] This then was an event of the greatest significance in the depth of her soul. Father Gracián, who as a priest at the altar was a vessel of Christ, would now fulfil the same function in the life of the saint as well.

Drawing on all the resources of her love, Teresa displays a constant motherly concern about the health and the spiritual progress of the treasured priest. The daughter in her exercises obedience. The woman gives her whole self in order (unexpectedly) to receive a greater, freer self in return. A breath of Eros blows through the whole, tender and elusive like the flight of the butterfly. But the impulse to it all comes from Teresa's union with God. That this is not impaired by the delegation to the 'representative' is shown both in her mystical writings—just at this point reaching completion—and in her visions, which reflect her inner stage of development. With her visionary inclination she is a child of her time—after all, even the sober holiness of an Ignatius of Loyola did not prevent him from being guided by visions in the founding of his Jesuit Order, for he recognised the will of God in them.

In Teresa's case, after her personal encounter with Father Jerónimo, particularly deep visionary (but imageless) experiences of God alternate harmoniously with imaginative Gracián-visions. Teresa gives precise accounts of them and identifies their meanings. She explains in *the Interior Castle* how deep centring is necessarily introduced by a vision of Christ which is then followed by imageless supernatural cognition of the divine Trinity and its 'indwelling'. She was familiar with participation in the loving life of the holy Trinity, but in August 1575, i.e. three months after the encounter in Beas, she had another illumination, in which God enabled her to perceive 'how the three Persons of the Blessed Trinity, which I bear imprinted in my soul, are one.'[5]

In this and in another vision that came right after it, the saint was absorbed in the question how the Son can have taken flesh and in what way he is present to the soul in communion. In these visions she begged Christ for guidance as to how she was to continue to cope with life on this earth, where she was not yet finally united to God, and received the answer: 'Think, daughter, of how after it [life] is finished you will not be able to serve me in ways you can now. Eat for Me and sleep for Me, and let everything you do be for Me, as though you no longer lived, but I; for this is what St Paul was speaking of.'[6]

These visionary insights into her inmost heart must be pondered in tandem with the letters quoted above, in which the saint acknowledges her human love.

The continual flow of Gracián-visions was viewed with a critical eye by both of the persons involved. One of these visions placed the father in a paradisal garden, but much too beautiful, with a garland of precious stones on his head, surrounded by singing virgins with palm branches in their hands ... and Teresa judges in conclusion: 'And what I drew from this was love for Eliseus and a remembrance of him in that beauty. I had feared lest it be a temptation, for it was impossible that it be the work of my imagination.'[7]

Gracián added:

> I too was fearful that we might be under the spell of a falsehood of the devil, for I am well aware how inferior I am to Mother Teresa in mind and soul, and how little I am worth. I have to say in addition that nobody desired the wellbeing and advancement of the Order of the Discalced Carmelites as much as I, and yet I had to endure numberless sufferings to prevent the founding statutes and rules of the Order of Mother Teresa from being changed by later Superiors who would come after me.

Gracián's personal affections were always interwoven with the wellbeing of the Order. When he presented his credentials on 21 November 1575, not only did Teresa raise the Presentation of Mary in the Temple to the rank of a high feast of the Order on that day, but she also received yet another vision. This time it was accepted:

> One night I was very distressed because it had been a long time since I had heard from my Father, and he had not been well when he last wrote. My affliction though was not like it had been when I first heard of his illness; for now I had confidence, and I was never as distressed as I had been the first time. But my concern hindered my prayer. He suddenly appeared to me, and in such a way that it couldn't have been my imagination. For a light appeared in the interior of my soul, and I beheld him coming along the road, happy and with a white countenance. Although by reason of the light by which I saw he had to have a white countenance, it seems to me that so do all those who are in heaven. And I wondered if the light and brilliance that comes from our Lord makes them white. I heard: 'Tell him to begin at once without fear, for his is the victory.[8]

How humanly close to us the great mystic seems to be here, when she cannot pray because of her loving anxiety! She continues: 'The day after he came, while I was praising our Lord at night for having granted me so many favours, the Lord said to me: "What do you ask of Me, my daughter, that I do not do?"'[9]

These examples show that her love for Father Jerónimo Gracián of the Mother of God did not drive any sort of wedge between Teresa and God. On the contrary: even the wedding symbolism of the first vision goes beyond the purely personal. Father Gracián speaks quite unselfconsciously about it:

Some of my opponents gave a thoroughly
shameful interpretation to the passage relating
how Christ put our hands together. In my
opinion however this union of the hands signi-
fied prophetic knowledge on the part of the
Mother. For from the day of our meeting in Beas
where Mother Teresa was granted the revelation mentioned and until the day of her death
we discussed and agreed on everything important, whether it had to do with the Order or
with personal matters.

Otger Steggink O.Carm. draws the conclusion:

By the way she integrated her womanliness into
this friendship, she showed that the psychological structure of human behaviour does not just
remain in place where there is a supernatural
love for God and man, but that it actually only
attains to its full development in that love.

Hand in hand

Father Gracián gives a very vivid description of how
he and Teresa would come to a common mind. There
is a note of delicate humour in this depiction, for
Gracián was all too aware on the one hand of the
superiority of his 'penitent', and yet on the other hand
he knew the dignity of his own priestly office too. No
simple situation for a prudent and sensitive man:

As her Superior I told her she had to think
everything through most carefully and then
commit it to God. If her opinion proved to differ
from mine, she must let me know, stick to it and
explain her reasons to me. Knowing and treas-
uring as I did her great prudence and holiness,
I would then give her view careful considera-

tion. In other cases she would hear my reasons
and follow my opinion. We frequently debated
and even argued about how issues ought to be
handled, but in the end we always reached a
common mind. Thus she was able to hang on
to that sense of obedience that mattered so
greatly to her.

Gracián, who never lost his healthy scepticism with
regard to visions, then put Mother Teresa to the test:

During our stay together in Beas the possibility
began to arise of founding a convent for nuns
in Madrid or Seville. It was not easy for me to
know which of these options appealed more to
the Mother. Therefore I asked her to confer with
our Lord about it. She spent three whole days
doing this and then said that the Lord had
declared himself for Madrid. I replied that we
needed to make a foundation in Seville, and she
accepted that. When I asked her why she had
not contradicted me, since it had been confirmed to her by many learned theologians that
the Spirit of God spoke through her, while my
decision had sprung purely from my personal
opinion, without my having prayed about it,
she answered: 'Faith tells me that everything
Your Reverence tells me to do springs from the
will of God, but I do not feel so confident about
my inner revelation.

It often happened to me that after a conversation with
her I reached some particular conclusion contrary to
hers, only to find myself changing my mind overnight.
When I then went to her and told her that what she
had proposed was definitely the best way forward, she
would smile. When I asked her why she was smiling,
her answer was that the Lord had already assured her

I would come round to her view. If her Superior
commanded her to do the opposite of what she considered right, then she would go to Our Lord and say
to him: 'Lord, if you agree with the view that I favour,
then change the heart of my Superior and make him
command it so that I can remain obedient to him.'

Teresa's obedience was therefore somewhat mis-
chievous. Father Gracián for his part thought up many
affectionate and somewhat humorous ways of sanctification and exercises in humility which satisfied the
saint's deep longing for inner progress. The story of
how the painter Juan de la Miseria came to paint her
portrait is well known, but existing narratives of it are
cryptically brief. Gracián's version however is meticulous as well as appreciative:

> Since I loved the holy Mother so much and
> knew that I could bring her the greatest joy with
> penitential exercises, I pondered carefully what
> I should impose on her without her dignity, her
> health, or her spirit suffering any damage from
> it. And so while we were staying in Seville, God
> gave me a sanctification exercise for her which
> I told her to carry out in connection with con-
> fession. It turned out to be one of the exercises
> that plagued her most. What I told her was that
> she must sit for a portrait. She found this very
> difficult indeed, since it involved attention
> being paid to her person—as if it were going to
> be important to hold on to the memory of her
> or talk about her noble origins. Anything like
> this struck her as quite undesirable, and I was
> very tempted to go back on the whole idea out
> of compassion for her, since she found the
> whole business so unpleasant, not least because
> I had strictly enjoined her to obey the painter,

Fray Juan de la Miseria. I was all too happy then
to keep my distance so as not to have to listen
to her objections and arguments against the
project. Fray Juan de la Miseria was frankly not
a great painter, he was neither as skilful nor as
courteous as others might have been. But one
day she turned up out of the blue on her way
to the monastery to ask him to paint her! He
prepared his colours and canvas and then had
her called. Not only had I subjected her to
obedience to him, but I had also laid him under
the duty of obedience to paint her as well as he
possibly could. He told her to put on the kind
of expression he wanted to see on her face and
scolded her when she could no longer keep
herself from laughing and started to lose the
expression. Still not satisfied, he took her face
in his hands and turned it to the light to get the
effect he desired. This whole exercise gave the
Mother scope for practising great patience, and
she indeed managed to hold on for a long time
without turning her head; in fact she put up
with the discomforts imposed on her in order
to make the painter's work easier. For all his
efforts, the end result was still a rather mediocre
likeness which showed none of the natural
charm and grace of the holy Mother's expression. She looked at the picture and commented:
'God forgive you Brother Juan—first you
plague the life out of me here and then to cap it
all you paint me looking so ugly and bleary-
eyed!' I am very glad to have told this story so
that nobody will assume that the holy Mother's
portrait was the product of even the merest
trace of vanity, since in reality it was all just a
penance laid on her!

The modern reader might suspect that Teresa's drive to penitential exercises could have had something to do with underlying masochistic tendencies. But the truth is that this would have been deeply alien to the moderation of the saint's outlook. 'I can only cope with the smallest sufferings' she wrote to the General of the Order. But she took her striving for perfection for the sake of the love of God extremely seriously. Hence at the time when she had resolved to pursue the reform of the Order, she had also made a vow of perfection. But it proved so difficult to carry out, that her Provincial at the time, Fray Angel de Salazar, amended it and mitigated it in the year 1565 at the behest of her confessor and of Mother Teresa herself. Her confessor Fray García de Toledo added the following clarificatory remarks:

> From this it follows that Your Reverence has to ask the father confessor whether anything serves the greater perfection or not. The path which the father confessor, who knows of your vows, declares to be the greater perfection, is the one you have to follow. In this connection however I must emphasise three preconditions: first, that your reverence consult her father confessor, second, that he be acquainted with the vow you have made and third, that he be the one to decide what is most perfect. Only under these three conditions will the vow be valid, otherwise not.[10]

It is clear that with a 'contract' like this, Teresa was dependent on her confessor's judgement, and this was scarcely any easier for her to endure than her previous scruples. It is quite understandable therefore that she was delighted to have found in Gracián such a discerning spiritual director with such a human understanding. Since she was however at least as concerned about his spiritual progress as about her own, and since it was necessary to find a balance between hierarchical superiority of office on the one hand and actual levels of spiritual attainment on the other, she asked Father Jerónimo to make a 'vow of perfection' too. Gracián mentions this in the autobiography he wrote in the form of a conversation. Cirilo asks Anastasio a question about one of the saint's writings:

> Cirilo: what is the meaning of these words in a letter of hers? 'I consider it a very great grace of God that Paul stands by his major decisions no matter how difficult things get, for this consistency of his means so much at those frequent periods when our peace is under threat from all sides. Thanks be to the One who endowed him with that quality! Your loyalty to our contract will be what reassures me, for ultimately all sufferings come to an end, and it wouldn't matter even if that were not so. You, my Father, know that I am carefully preserving this document so that I can hold you to it if you fail to keep your side. The moment is highly propitious, for I am concerned right now that Paul should do nothing to misrepresent the will of God. But Joseph has assured Angela that all will go well and that Paul will continue to be more and more pleasing to God.
>
> Anastasio: Here Mother Teresa calls herself Angela, Christ is called Joseph and she calls Anastasio Paul. You need to be aware that I always reported to her in my letters whatever was happening in my soul when we were apart. I frequently managed to fill whole notebooks

in this way and she used to keep them. In times
of conflict and confusion, the Lord gave me the
idea of promising Mother Teresa of Jesus that I
would always do what was most pleasing to
God in everything, and I gave her my word to
hold fast to this in the future. I pondered
making an official vow, but I was counselled
not to do so for fear of falling into scrupulous-
ness. I was advised to make a firm promise
instead, so I wrote one out in the form of a
contract and gave it to Mother Teresa. From
then on I found that my desire always to do
what was most pleasing to God grew stronger
and stronger. I believe this is what Mother
Teresa was referring to in her letter!

Leading and led

Each of them then was both leading the other and
being led by the other. The 'obedient daughter' gave
way again and again to the solicitous mother and the
saint demonstrated her instinctive concern for the
body as well as for the soul. A few examples may
prove this:

> What does surprise me is that, in spite of all he
> has to do, Paul can commune with Joseph so
> tranquilly. I give hearty praise to the Lord. Your
> Paternity should tell Paul to be perfectly content
> now with his prayer and not to trouble about
> performing acts with his understanding when
> God grants him favours of another kind; and
> you should say that I am very happy about
> what he writes to me. The fact is that, in these
> interior, spiritual things, the most potent and
> acceptable prayer is the prayer that leaves the
> best effects. I do not mean it must immediately
> fill the soul with desires; for although such

desires are good, they are sometimes not as good as our love of self makes us think. I should describe the best effects as those that are followed up by actions—when the soul not only desires the honour of God, but really strives for it, and employs the memory and understanding in considering how it may please Him and show its love for Him more and more.

Oh, that is real prayer—which cannot be said of a handful of consolations that do nothing but console ourselves. When the soul experiences these, they leave it weak and fearful and sensitive to what others think of it. I should never want any prayer that would not make the virtues grow within me. If with my prayer there come severe temptations and aridity and tribulations, and these leave me humbler, then I should consider it good prayer, for by the best prayer I mean that which is most pleasing to God. One must not think that a person who is suffering is not praying. He is offering up his sufferings to God, and many a time he is praying much more truly than one who goes away by himself and meditates his head off, and, if he has squeezed out a few tears, thinks that that is prayer.

Your Paternity must forgive my asking you to convey such a long message. Your love for Paul will serve as my excuse. If you think what I have said is good, you must pass it on to him; if not, don't. I am just telling you my own feelings about it. I assure you there are two great things—works and a clear conscience.[11]

Although Teresa's warning against the craving for spiritual pleasure may have influenced the young

Gracián, the truth is that at the deepest level he had no inclination for it anyway. Later he wrote: 'Those who set their hearts on following the best and surest way must never look for inner happiness or personal uplift in prayer, they must rather desire nothing but the cross.'

And then, as a personal confession when talking to Cirilo in the *Pilgrimage of Anastasio*:

> I have experienced inner darkness; the torments of self-reproach and deeply disheartening anxieties; despairing depression and the kind of stress that makes the soul feel as though it is going to suffocate; an untimely zeal that eats away at the heart; inward and outward desolation; monstrous temptations, threatening situations, aridities, and the like. That is all you need to know, do not ask me any more questions, for I find it very hard to put my heart on display like this.

And:

> I have prayed to God for a cross and suffering ever since I first developed a prayer life at the age of twenty. I begged God time and again to divert me from the way of wealth and from those honours whether worldly or spiritual that are so often lavished on men of learning. I have also asked him not to give me the kind of visions, revelations, and miracles that tend to encourage people to look on a person as some kind of saint. Instead of all this I asked only for the naked and shameful cross, recognising the right and sure way to heaven in that.

When Teresa heard that Gracián had safely arrived in Seville in October 1576, she wrote to him:

God be blessed for this, and also that Paul is
well and is enjoying inward tranquillity. He is
making such very great progress that it really
seems like something supernatural; this nature
of ours must need all these (trials), so far do
they go towards humiliating us and giving us
self-knowledge. For a long time I have been
praying to the Lord here to grant him such a
period of calm, as it seemed to me that he had
enough troubles already: will your Paternity
tell him so for me?[12]

In her enthusiasm Teresa has dropped her 'Paul'
fiction here but she very quickly takes it up again!
Father Gracián's sleeplessness and headaches, aggra-
vated by his over-long prayers, cause her great anxiety.

I assure you Joseph is right to let you sleep. I
was delighted to hear it, for, since your Paternity left, I have been begging and beseeching
Him most earnestly to do so, as it seemed to me
absolutely necessary. It almost looked as if He
had been doing it for me, and I really believe
now that He has done it because I have been
praying for it so hard. If you can sleep like that
you will get through your work.[13]

I have just re-read Paul's letter, in which he says
he is unable to sleep because he is making
plans—I think he means to become absorbed in
prayer. Your Paternity must tell him not to get
into the habit of giving up such a priceless boon
except for one reason—namely, so as not to rob
himself of sleep, which his body needs—for the
blessings which the Lord gives in prayer are of
great price and I should not be surprised if the
devil were attempting to deprive him of them.[14]

I assure you, my Father, it will be a good thing if your Paternity can sleep. You see, you have a lot of work to do and, until your head gets into a hopeless state, you do not realize how you are overtaxing your strength. And you know how important it is that you should be well. So, for the love of God, look at the thing from another point of view, and stop devoting the hours in which you ought to be asleep either to making plans—however necessary they may be—or to prayer. Please do this out of kindness to me, for often, when the devil sees that someone is very fervent in spirit, he keeps drawing his attention to things which seem of great importance for the service of God, so that if he cannot prevent good being done in one way, he will do so in another ...[15]

Teresa's exhortations fell on fruitful ground, as Gracián explained much later:

When God sends illness and pains, and the soul accepts these gently and patiently and receives them thankfully as great graces that keep alive the thought of the pains of the crucified one, then for many persons illnesses become the cause of spiritual growth through participation in the cross. If however a person refuses to obey the instructions of the doctor and his superiors, damaging his health for the sake of keeping up appearances in that he does not want people inside or outside the monastery to look on the illness as a setback for him—he will be punished by God. His mental state will be weakened and inner and outer peace will be denied him. Therefore David says: *Fortitudinem meam ad te custodiam*.[16] There is no question that great spiritual and bodily strength is essential if we

are to stand firm amid the torrent of pain and
love which the true spiritual (mystical) life
brings with it. Anyone who wants to grow in
that life should take it from me that where his
health is concerned he must obey his doctors
and his superiors, for God not only made
medicine in heaven but He also made the
prudent man who treats it with respect.

Teresa's concern extended to include practical meas-
ures. In the friary of Los Remedios the cooking was
evidently not of a kind to suit a sensitive stomach.
Even worse, Teresa, ever the realist, worried that the
friars might try to poison Gracián out of envy and
hatred, following a practice that would not have been
greatly out of the ordinary at the time. So it was that
she told Gracián—whose additional responsibilities
since 21 November for so many friaries of the Calced
meant that he was often travelling and vulnerable to
hostile actions—not to take his meals just anywhere
but only in the convent of nuns in Seville, to whose
prioress Teresa was close. This instruction conflicted
with Teresa's other principles and rules, something
that embroiled her in constant conflict, as several
letters show. For example she wrote to the Prioress
Maria de San José: 'Don't be remiss about it and see
that you look after our Father occasionally. He strongly
supports our opinion that no friars must be allowed
there. We have gone into this again and again and I
should not like him to be too extreme, in view of his
needs and of the importance to us of keeping him
well.'[17]

Three months later (Gracián having in the meantime
presented his Brief), without naming names Teresa

once again warned against the food in the priories. She wrote to him:

> Jesus be with your Paternity, my Father. Whenever, as so often happens, I get a letter from your Paternity, I wish I could kiss your hands once more; I do not know what I should have done in this place you left me in without such consolation. May God be blessed for everything...
>
> However it comes about, I trust in God that everything will turn out well, for He is turning Paul into a regular enchanter...
>
> I have (always) had the deepest affection for the nuns at Seville, and I love them more every day for the care they are taking of one whom I wish I could be always cherishing and serving and taking care of too. God be praised for granting him such good health. But, for the love of God, never be off your guard as to what you eat in those houses (of the Observance).
>
> I am well, and happy at getting news of your Paternity so often. May His Majesty watch over you for me and make you as holy as I pray Him to do. Amen.[18]

Gracián commented somewhat dramatically on all this:

> I always wore a bezoar stone[19] around my neck when I ate in the priories I visited, and I also took great care not to eat anything but boiled eggs served to me in their shells. But the truth is that any food tastes dreadful when it is flavoured with the sauce of a fear of what is being eaten. One day one of my companions found a newt in the water jug out of which we drank. It could not have got in there by itself.

Teresa was then more than justified in her anxieties
and in the exceptions she made to rules. But Father
Gracián was also lovingly concerned about her, and
his solicitude certainly did not limit itself to carefully
considered penitential exercises, as the following letter
shows:

> May the Grace of the Holy Spirit be with your
> Paternity, my Father. Oh, what benedictions
> this old daughter of yours called down on you
> for this letter which I received from Father
> Mariano today, the ninth of January! ...
>
> It is extremely fortunate that the second letter
> arrived so quickly; each day your Paternity puts
> me under a deeper obligation by your concern
> for my happiness, and I trust in God that He
> will repay you...
>
> Oh, how happy Angela felt when she read the
> sentiments which he expresses on a separate
> sheet at the end of one of the letters which he
> wrote her! She says she would like to kiss his
> hands many times and your Paternity is to tell
> him that he can be quite easy about it in his
> mind, since the work of bringing about the
> union was so well done, and the knot was so
> tightly tied, that only death will break it—nay,
> after death it will be firmer than before, and no
> foolish notions about perfection could do as
> much as that; the very thought of it helps her to
> praise the Lord. That freedom which she used
> to have has been nothing but a hindrance to her.
> Now she thinks her present bondage better and
> more pleasing to God, for she has found
> someone to help her bring souls to Him who
> will praise Him. And such is the relief and joy
> which overflows in her that a large part of it

spreads to me. May He be blessed for everything.

Your Paternity's unworthy daughter and subject,

Teresa of Jesus.[20]

The kiss on the hand was a gesture commonly offered by women to spiritual dignitaries. In Teresa's letters it was accorded to other addressees too. The saint had a deep understanding of the 'wedding' aspect of her great Gracián-vision, and it led her to develop her inner relationship to freedom and 'submission' as a part of her aspiration to perfection. A feminine need for self-giving fused indistinguishably with the spirit of monastic obedience like 'rain with a river', as Teresa had said about the *Unio mystica*, union with God. The initial excitement of this letter of love, this thanksgiving for the love of Father Gracián, dies away again into joyful thoughts of their shared apostolate, or, as we would say today, their missionary task.

Aware of her responsibility to this partner thirty years her junior, Teresa applied herself unstintingly to the role of being an educator for him. In fact this merely amounted to a *quid pro quo* corresponding to the sanctification practices that he habitually imposed on her. She wrote:

> I want to tell you of something I was tempted to wonder about Eliseus yesterday: it is still troubling me. I was wondering if he is not rather careless sometimes in telling the whole truth about everything. I realize the things concerned will be quite unimportant, but I should like him to be extremely careful about it. Will your Paternity please put this to him

very seriously from me, for I do not believe
there can be absolute perfection where there is
carelessness, about that? Just see how I meddle
in these things, as if I had nothing else to
concern me.

Will your Paternity be sure to commend me to
God? I badly need your prayers.[21]

In a much more personal vein she writes:

May the grace of the Holy Spirit be with your
Paternity...

... as she herself says, she (Teresa) has a great
many trials and is weak by nature, so that she
becomes distressed when she thinks (her affection) is not repaid. Your Paternity must please
tell that gentleman (Gracián) that, careless
though he may be by nature, he must not be so
with her; for, where there is love, it cannot
slumber so long...

I am reasonably well. The Prioress and the
sisters here wish to be warmly remembered to
your Paternity. God protect you and let me see
you soon — it is past three o'clock.[22]

Teresa's practical sense shied away from no
details where improvements were concerned:

I am afraid that this little mule is not the right
sort for your Paternity; I think you had better
buy a good one. If you do that, you will easily
find someone to lend you the money, and, when
I am paid here, I will send you some ...

The only thing I am afraid of is that a beast may
be bought that will throw my Father, whereas

> I am not worried about his falling off the mule,
> as it is so small.[23]

Teresa was quite right to be concerned about Father Gracián's riding skills, for this scholarly man was the very opposite of the sporting type. Teresa had already written to him in October 1575: 'I must tell you that I am cross about these falls you have been having. It would be as well if they were to tie you onto your mount, and then you could not fall. I don't know what sort of a donkey you have, nor why your Paternity has to do ten leagues a day; on a pack-saddle that is suicidal.'[24]

Gracián accepted this criticism humbly and expressed great admiration for Teresa's own riding skills:

> The Mother's careful attention to everything needed by those travelling with her was something to see. You would have thought she had nothing else to think about and had been a mule driver all her life! She would frequently call over to her people who had to go on foot, comforting them and conversing so charmingly with them that they were wholly distracted from their tiredness. She was such a good rider that she was quite capable of carrying on talking about God and the things of religious life as if she was sitting comfortably in a coach, when in fact she was actually riding on a mule. On one occasion her hinny took fright and bolted with her on it, but she showed not an ounce of fear and quickly brought the animal under control without the least sign of the kind of panic that one often sees with women in such situations. We can only conclude that God gave her the grace for everything—and especially for all the

endless travelling which she undertook under
His guidance and for His praise and glory.

Riding skills are of course no requirement for holiness,
yet given the amount of travelling she did in the
service of the reform of the Order, Teresa's ability to
ride well was as crucial for her as the ability to drive
is in our day.

While Teresa worried a great deal about Father
Gracián's health and safety, she was at the same time
quite happy to help toughen him up in the service of
their shared mission. She was equally happy to pass
unfavourable comment on his other human weak-
nesses (as in the letters cited): her criticism was tender
and careful but it was also trenchant. Father Gracián's
own assessment of himself was however even harsher.
In a letter to Discalced Carmelites of 22 October 1577
in which he sought to console them in the persecutions
they were suffering while apologising that his appointment as Visitor had led to so many troubles, he added
at the end: 'If I was the only one they were slandering,
I would really feel quite cheerful about it and quite
happy to thank those responsible for reminding me of
the thoughtlessness of my self-love, something which
my mistakes and bad habits encourage me to forget.'

In his later autobiography Father Gracián only
reported Teresa's obedience to him after he had made
a point of expounding on his own unworthiness under
twelve heads.

Such was the view of himself held by this man
whose life was a sacrifice to his own almost childlike
openness and carefree outlook. The historian of the
Order, Father Silverio de Santa Teresa OCD, quotes
with enthusiasm from the work of a Discalced Carmelite, Fray Antonio de los Reyes, who at the end of

the eighteenth century wrote about Jerónimo Grácian in the following terms:

> Father Gracián was a man of great purity and innocence in his dealings with persons of the opposite sex, so much so that many people thought his gentle kindness to be overly free and easy. It is hardly surprising that some took note of this and later used it as ammunition against him ... our holy Mother came to the conclusion that that this free and easy familiarity so typical of Father Gracián was that of a saint[25], but she was anxious to forestall the malicious interpretations and suspicions provoked by his uninhibited behaviour.

Nuncio Ormaneto, who supported the reform, also valued Father Gracián very highly, and he wrote on 4 March 1577 'that those who speak ill of Father Gracián are very poorly informed and indeed quite mistaken. For this friar leads a very upright life of great holiness and shows a huge capacity to deal with all the affairs of the Order.'

Notes

1 Ps 147, 14, 'He maintains the peace of your frontiers'.
2 *Spiritual Testimonies* 36, i/ii/iii/iv, Beas, April 1575 in *CW* i, 338.
3 *Spiritual Testimonies* 36 in *CW* i, 340.
4 *Spiritual Testimonies* 36 in *CW* i, 340.
5 *Spiritual Testimonies* 42, Aug 28 1575 in *CW* i, 343.
6 *Spiritual Testimonies* 52, 1575 in *CW* i, 346.
7 *Spiriutal Testimonies* 39 in *CW* i, 342.
8 In Spanish the last sentence has a double meaning and is mostly applicable to Teresa. The final situation, however, as pp. 306ff of the autobiography of P Gracián (Burgos 1905) shows, is more connected with the battles in the Order involving Gracián. See *Spiritual Testimonies* no 54, 1575 in *CW* i, 347.

9   *Spiritual Testimonies* no 54, 1575 in CW i, 348.
10   Fray García de Toledo, Toledo, 2 March 1565.
11   *Letters* I, 316 no 122, 23 Oct 1576.
12   *Letters* I, 293 no 114, 5 October 1576.
13   *Letters* I, 485 no 212 Oct 1577 [?].
14   *Letters* I, 508 no 225 Dec 1577 [?].
15   *Letters* I, 495 no 220 Dec 1577 [?].
16   'My strength, it is you to whom I turn' Ps 58:10. Translator's note: The German text here is closer to the Vulgate—translating 'Lord, I want to preserve my health and strength for you.'
17   *Letters* I, 276 no 107, 7 Sept 1576.
18   *Letters* I, 364 no 145, 7 Dec 1576.
19   In both editions *piedra basar* meaning *bezoar*—shortened to *bezar*. Translator's note: Bezoar stone = from the liver of animals, regarded as a cure for ailments.
20   *Letters* I, 399 no 160, 9 Jan 1577.
21   *Letters* II, 673 no 283, 18 Jul 1579.
22   *Letters* II, 683/686 no 290, 4 Oct 1579.
23   *Letters* II, 775 no 333, 4 Oct 1580.
24   *Letters* I, 202 no 81, Oct 1575.
25   See the letter of 16 Dec 1577 in the chapter above 'The best days of my life'.

5

WAR IN CARMEL

A Campaign of slander

MANY OBSERVERS WERE understandably horrified by the movement for Reform from the very start, dismissing it as completely unacceptable that a woman and a greenhorn young friar should set out to reform the venerable Order of the Carmelites! Suspicions were only intensified by their openly-acknowledged personal relationship—which inevitably opened the door wide to envy and plain and simple misunderstanding. On top of this Gracián made up his mind—in the teeth of the anger of the General of the Order and against the instincts (i.e. the vision) of Teresa—to found a further priory in Seville.

An initial spell of pure gossip and rumbling discontent gradually ramped up to a deliberate campaign of hostility and slander. The members of the 'Calced' Order were now beginning to look for trouble. While Teresa was still sunning herself in her new friendship, with its huge potential to contribute to the Reform, opponents were gathering their forces for an attack. A General Chapter in Italy (Piacenza) under the presidency of the incensed General of the Order (Rubeo) had been called for 22 May 1575. Teresa complains in her book of the Foundations:

> That which came about next did so either because His Majesty desired to give me some rest or because the devil was displeased that so

many houses were being founded where our
Lord was being served. (It was easy to understand that what came about was not the will of
our Father General because he had written me
not many years before in answer to my request
not to found any more houses that he would
not stop ordering me to do so because he
wanted me to make as many foundations as I
had hairs on my head.) Before I came back from
Seville, a general chapter was held. In a general
chapter one would think they would be concerned about the expansion of the order, but
instead the definitory gave me a command not
merely to make no more foundations but not to
leave the house in which I chose to reside,
which would be a kind of prison, for there is no
nun who for necessary matters pertaining to the
good of the order cannot be ordered by the
provincial to go from one place to another, I
mean from one monastery to another. And what
was worse and what made me sad was that our
Father General was displeased with me,
without any reason at all, because of information given by biased persons.[1]

Nonetheless Teresa managed to put a positive slant on
this new turn of events and share some useful teaching
with her Sisters:

Along with this I was told of two other serious
calumnies that were raised against me. I tell
you, Sisters, so that you will see the mercy of
our Lord and how His Majesty does not
abandon the one who desires to serve Him. For
these calumnies not only failed to make me sad
but gave me so great an accidental joy[2] that I
could not restrain myself. As a result, I'm not
surprised at what David did when he went

before the Ark of the Lord, for because of my joy which I didn't know how to conceal I wanted to do nothing else at the time. I don't know the reason, for this has never happened to me in all the other great criticism and opposition I have received. Moreover, one of these two calumnies spoken against me was most serious. But the command not to make foundations—aside from the displeasure of our Most Reverend Father General—brought me great tranquillity and was what I was often desiring; to end my days in quiet. But this was not what those who devised this were intending. They wanted to inflict on me the greatest sorrow in the world, and perhaps they may have had other good intentions.

On occasion, also, the strong opposition and criticism (sometimes offered with good intentions and at other times for other purposes) that I received in making these foundations gave me great joy. But I don't ever remember, no matter how much the hardship, experiencing happiness as great as I did in this instance...

I believe that my main joy came from my thinking that since creatures repaid me like this I was pleasing the Creator. For I am convinced that he who looks for joy in earthly things or in words of praise from men is very much mistaken, without mentioning the little advantage there is in them. Today people will think one thing, tomorrow another; at one time they will speak well of something; soon they will speak badly of it. May you be blessed, my Lord and my God, for You are unchangeable forever and ever, amen. The one who serves unto the end will live without end in Your eternity.[3]

Teresa's best friend, Prioress Maria de San José, in whose convent in Seville Father Gracián usually took his meals, gave a careful and sober explanation of events :

> The main cause of the troubles was that our Mother fell into disfavour with the Most Reverend General because she wanted to make foundations in Andalusia. He was very put out by her foundation journey to Seville and still more by the fact that she had gone there on Gracián's instructions. He was very annoyed with the latter for having begun visitations in Andalusia without consulting him. He ended up bearing a grudge against all the Discalced, and the Calced were not slow to exploit the situation. They told him that the breakaway movement and consequent decline in the Order was—as they saw it—our Mother's fault. At the same time they reproached the General for having given the foundation licence for new convents, which they alleged had encouraged the Mother and the other Discalced to rebel against him and withdraw their obedience towards him. This kind of talk so embittered the General against our Mother that neither her letters nor any other peace feelers could placate him. In the end things reached a point that the General Chapter had to be summoned. It accused all the Discalced of disobedience and excommunicated them. Entire convents founded without the permission of the General were to be closed, namely those in Seville, Granada, Almodóvar, and Perinela. The Chapter desired further that our Mother be stripped of authority to make foundations and that she should be confined to one convent and not allowed to leave it. The

Discalced were to start wearing shoes again and use melodies in their singing (for Teresa recommended recitation on a single note), and so forth. It is quite appalling that so holy a man as our Father General and other worthy fathers and servants of God could come to such an unreasonable decision as that convents should be closed when they had only just been founded—and on apostolic authority at that.

When Father Gracián came to Seville with the Nuncio's Brief—which was not something he had been looking for at all—and wanted to exercise his office as Visitator, the Calced were so angry that they threatened armed resistance when he tried to oblige them to obedience. There was such a tumult that Mother Teresa—who was at that point absorbed in prayer with her nuns—was informed that Father Gracián had been murdered, that the doors were locked, and that there was an almighty racket. The Mother began to panic but our Lord then spoke to her: 'O you of little faith! Calm down, for all will be well!'

Maria de San José writes of further slanders which then resulted in Teresa and her nuns being summoned before the Inquisition. They had been denounced by a novice who had been refused acceptance into the Order. The report alleged that they were sectaries (*alumbrados*) and claimed they were guilty of monastic irregularities. Teresa had wanted to obey the injunction to withdraw to a cloister in Castile at once, but Gracián's counter-injunction and also the necessity of not running away from the Inquisition induced her to remain longer in Seville. Prudently, she wrote to the General to tell him she was staying on for the sake of her health, which did not allow her to travel in the winter. Further difficulties with an emotionally dis-

turbed priest in Seville plus fresh denunciations added
to her burdens, but the Inquisitors very soon realised
that 'we should leave the vein that has no blood in it
alone'.

The slanderous gossip continued however, and it
left its mark—as it always does. Maria de San José
reported that the fathers levelled charges against
Mother Teresa 'in which the dirtiest and most disgust-
ing words were used, which my clean pen refuses to
write down.' The least indecent claim was a statement
by many witnesses that 'the old cousin' (Teresa) was
using the founding of monasteries merely as a pretext
to introduce young girls to loose living. When the holy
Mother read this accusation, all she said was: 'It is a
good thing that when they feel obliged to lie, they do
it in such a way that one can only shake one's head
and laugh.'

Our chronicler, Prioress Maria de San José, was then
herself dragged into the campaign of defamation,
being accused of an illegitimate relationship with
Father Gracián. Her sole response was to express
regret that such an affront could be offered 'to the holy
man that Father Jerónimo Gracián was'.

Gracián later wrote a letter of apology (which gives
a hint of his fascinating preaching style) to Teresa's
nuns for having been the cause of their suffering such
slanders and persecutions for his sake. He writes:

> A disciple of the Apostle Paul named Hermas
> describes a vision to us. He relates how ... a
> dust storm blew up to the sky, and out of it
> came a creature bigger than a whale with a
> hundred feet, it was hurling tongues of fire out
> of its mouth and it had a head of four colours—
> black, red, gold, and white. In its monstrous

fury it looked as though it was about to destroy a city. But when Hermas approached the monster, he found that all it could do was make rapid movements of its tongue. Thirty paces beyond it he came face to face with a very beautiful young girl dressed all in white. Although she was very young, nonetheless her hair was all white like that of an old woman, and she asked him 'what did you see, Hermas?' and she added: 'know that I am the Church and I will explain what you have seen, for although I have the beauty and vigour of a young girl, the hairs of my thoughts are very wise.

This monster is slander. It has a hundred feet because it is never short of evil men to proceed against the good, and its mouth breathes a consuming fire that will blacken your honour. The blackness on the head points to the deception and the tricks it intends to use to bring about your downfall; the redness is for the rage that drives it to crave the blood of the just: they are tried like gold in the tribulations of persecution so that they can enter into the pearly white brightness of glory. Don't be afraid of the creature, it really can't do anything but move its tongue. Woe to those who waver in times of persecution, it would be better for them not to have been born! ...

Blessed are they, says the Lord, who suffer persecution and his Apostle adds: 'if we bless those who persecute us...'

My sisters, in the face of your perpetual enclosure and the rule that does not allow even other family members to see your faces, God allows you to be slandered as loose-living; in the face of your hard ascetic discipline, you are considered sensual; in the face of your silence and perpetual prayer in the presence of God, you are reproached for idleness. In return for your striving for perpetual purification and mortification you are thought to behave lecherously and provocatively. I am more than happy to witness your lot in this world because I recognise in it the crown of victory which is promised to you for all eternity. Nonetheless I am deeply sorry that I myself should be the occasion of all these persecutions; I can see that in this reform rivalries are unavoidable, even though they are purely the result of obedience to the Nuncio and the command of the King. So I beg you from the bottom of my heart to forgive me for the sake of the mercy of Jesus Christ...

Jerónimo Fray de la Madre de Dios.

Father Gracián reports the slanders to which he himself was subjected at this time in the 'Pilgrim journeys of Anastasio'. Here is a short extract:

It has always been my practice to keep a picture of the holy Virgin in my scapular for the night-time. Consequently they spread it about that I slept with pictures of our dear Lady, insinuating to those who heard about this the most frightful and damnable blasphemy. Once when I was absent for a short while for the purposes of a visitation, they announced publicly from the chancel of the monastery at Seville that now all the wickedness and abuses of 'this bad man' had been brought to light, I had been condemned to the flames, and a written certificate would be sent with my ashes.

Teresa wrote to Gracián:

Although it has really caused me great distress,
I have also been deeply affected to learn of the
tact which your Paternity has shown amidst so
much slander. I assure you, my Father, God has
a great love for you and you are walking in
close imitation of Him. Be very glad, for He is
giving you what you are asking of Him—
namely, trials—and since He is just He will
defend you. May He be blessed for ever.[4]

The Interior Castle

On 4 June 1576 Teresa left Seville. She had remained
well over a year in Andalusia, a place for which she
had never had much liking. She would have preferred
to go to Valladolid, but Gracián, severe now in his role
as office-bearer, directed her to head for Toledo. After
a few stops in between, she reached there on 23 June.
In an enforced though pleasant interval she wrote
more letters than ever. The first ones still resounded
with the confusing experiences she had been through.
But after just four weeks of settling in, she reported to
her brother Lorenzo: 'Personally, I think I am better
than I have been for years, and I have a very nice cell,
extremely secluded, with a window overlooking the
garden. I am not kept busy with visitors.'[5]

At the end of August Father Gracián received news
from her: 'The method of visiting Discalced nuns is
such that it might have been taught by God. May He
be blessed for everything.'[6]

This may sound very mysterious, but in fact Teresa
had written an uncommonly clear and prudent treatise
on the conduct of visitations. In her 'exile' she worked
away in perfect serenity on the future of her Order,
drawing up very concrete rules for the way that
visitations should be conducted. In this she was guided

by the model provided by Father Gracián and by her desire to relay to her contemporaries and to posterity his huge prudence, integrity, and giftedness for the Order. She emphasises the combination of mildness and severity that was so characteristic of him, tending to lay the stress on the severity—perhaps also as an indirect way of giving Gracián advice. She gives hints for life in the cloister out of her own experience, and especially out of the bitter experiences of the preceding months. She warns against overrating the prioresses and against excessively friendly relationships between nuns and their confessors. She writes:

> It is necessary that future Visitators follow what is done now by the provincial that the Lord has given us. I have taken much of what I've said here from observing his visitations, especially the following point: he shows no more familiarity to one Sister (in such a way that he spends time alone with her or writes to her) than he does to all, but he shows love to all together as a true father. The day in which a visitator in some monastery should have a particular friendship, even though it may be like that between St Jerome and St Paula, he will not escape the critical remarks of others, anymore than those two did. And not only will it do harm in that monastery but in all of them, for the devil will at once make it known so as to gain something. Because of our sins the world has gone so astray in this respect that many troubles arise, as is now seen…

> This does not refer to times in which necessity may require some special attention, but to things that are noticeable and excessive.[7]

The last sentence, which mentions the exception to the rules prescribed, reveals Teresa's conflicted state. She knows that her particular personal relationship and her exchange of letters cannot be a norm for all nuns, and she is honourable enough not to found the exception she makes for herself solely on the necessities of the Order, but ultimately on her human maturity and closeness to God. One year later she had finally managed to come to the calm statement 'I can allow it for myself'. Great prudence and warmth lie behind her austere words on the conduct of visitations: no hint of a doubt about the admissibility and pleasingness to God of the love of a St Jerome and his St Paula. But there is at the same time an awareness of the evil in the world which loves to blacken the radiant and to drag the sublime into the dust, along with an awareness of the bad consequences of the foolish or malicious gossip which so poisons the atmosphere.

Teresa had composed the visitation text at Gracián's behest straight after her arrival in Toledo. At his prompting she also again resumed work on her interrupted series of reports about her foundations. She did this all the more willingly in that she was still humming with the excitement of their encounter in Beas and their sharing in Andalusia. Her letters expressed hopes of a swift reunion.

Yet the one she loved so much made her wait eleven months for him. He could not do otherwise, for scarcely comprehensible battles were raging outside, challenging him and forcing him to become involved. He did not finally reach Toledo until 28 May 1577. They were soon buried in profound conversations like the ones they had had earlier in Beas, a spiritual soul-deep exchange, far more significant than any worldly hustle and bustle. The convent in Toledo became a fortress, a castle, into whose innermost fastness only love could penetrate. Out of this 'dialogue with a friend, who we know loves us' grew the plan for Teresa's greatest work, the *Interior Castle*. A mystical guidebook, as significant as the *Ascent of Mount Carmel* of St John of the Cross and conveying the mystical experience perhaps even more powerfully. When Gracián 'commanded' Mother Teresa to write *The Interior Castle*, he must have sensed that this monumental work had come to maturity in her soul like a fruit that had ripened. The task was a gift, an unutterable joy. She wrote the book in a state of quasi-intoxication in the space of eight (frequently interrupted) weeks. To begin with she had of course raised all her customary objections, which Father Gracián reports on as follows:

> So when I visited Mother Teresa during her enforced pause in Toledo, I persuaded her by dint of a great deal of pestering to write the book which she was to entitle *Las Moradas* ('the Dwellings'). She threw up endless arguments in the face of my insistence, repeating what she already said elsewhere, namely: 'Why should I be the one to write? Let those who have studied and those who have some understanding of things be the ones to do it. I am but a fool who does not know what she says and who does a lot of damage by a bad choice of words. Anyway, quite enough books have been written on prayer. For God's sake, leave me to sit at my spinning wheel and do my other duties and keep the hours of prayer like all the other sisters do. I am not made for writing, neither my health nor my head are up to it, etc.' It was only with

a parable that I could convince her: I talked to her about healing practitioners who gained their prescriptions from experience, like Hippocrates, Galen, and others of importance in the sphere of medicine, pointing out that what was valid in the sphere of the care of the body also applied to care of the soul. For those who strive after a life of prayer and spiritual progress can learn just as much from writings based on experience as they can from studies written by the learned. I suggested a comparison with a traveller faced with the necessity of going down a dangerous road with tricky bends and gorges. Where would such a person go for advice? From someone who had already gone down the road once and knew from experience where the dangers lay, or from someone who wrote very eloquently about the danger points purely on the basis of hearsay, without ever having seen them for himself? It is no different with souls who follow the rough and steep paths of prayer. In the end, prayer comes down to doing and practising and accomplishment through activity, all this is much better explained by the person who possesses experience of it than by the mere theoretician.

Mother Teresa's style is particularly suited to exposition of the whole truth in its naked simplicity, without rhetorical devices, affectation, or distortions. Moreover a careful study of her writing style reveals how superbly appropriate it is as an instrument for convincing and persuading. She writes as elegantly as anyone in the history of Spanish literature. Even after laborious revision and correction few scholars and writers are capable of writing such logical and internally coherent sentences, whereas in fact Mother Teresa wrote at great speed and without crossing anything out or changing anything. There is a clarity in her style not always found in woman writers, and she writes as fluently and rapidly as only notaries usually manage to do. Moreover I was perpetually astonished at the sheer number of letters she wrote every day in her own hand and sent to her monasteries. No nun remained without an answer to her letter, nor for that matter did anyone else—if it was a question of the affairs of the Order or an inquiry or doubt with respect to prayer. Where the choice of words is concerned, her thoughts are so always clearly expressed that one knows exactly what she wants to say, and it hardly matters what actual words she uses.

What she says invariably turns out to be true and it is understood by readers just as she intended it to be.

Teresa reached the apogee of her abilities and experience in *The Interior Castle*. She had no need to make apologies or follow models. In the allegory of the castle, with its basis in the Bible, she presents us with an expression of the deepest knowledge of her heart accomplished with immense literary skill:

Today while beseeching Our Lord to speak for me because I wasn't able to think of anything to say nor did I know how to begin to carry out this obedience, there came to my mind what I shall now speak about, that which will provide us with a basis to begin with. It is that we consider our soul to be like a castle made entirely out of a diamond or of very clear crystal, in which there are many rooms, just as in heaven there are many dwelling-places. For in reflecting upon it carefully, Sisters, we realize that the soul of the just person is nothing else but a paradise where the Lord says He finds his delight...

Well, let us consider that this castle has, as I said, many dwelling-places; some up above, others down below, others to the sides; and in the centre and middle is the main dwelling-place where the very secret exchanges between God and the soul take place.

It is necessary that you keep this comparison in mind.[8]

Father Gracián played a huge part in all of this. What moving conversations must have preceded the composition of this chapter, which has a dynamic all of its own! Although Teresa often writes 'more theologically' in this work than in her others—which may be a reflection of the presence of Father Gracián—every bit of theory takes her back into the depths of experience. Thus after the exploration of the being of the divine Trinity, into whose life the person who has reached the seventh dwelling is taken up, comes the observation:

Oh, God help me! How different is hearing and believing these words from understanding their truth in this way! Each day this soul becomes more amazed, for these Persons never seem to leave it any more, but it clearly beholds, in the way that was mentioned, that they are within it. In the extreme interior, in some place very deep within itself, the nature of which it doesn't know how to explain, because of a lack of learning, it perceives this divine company.[9]

The experiences and the writings that came out of this week stayed fresh in the depths of Gracián's heart throughout the rest of his life. He too sought to give graphic expression to the event of being received into the love of God and to portray something of the sense of being inwardly overwhelmed. In doing so he connected with the work of Saint Teresa as well as with the vision of the Apostle Paul, who saw himself transported into the third heaven. Gracián writes:

> My heart flutters and my tongue freezes when I have to portray the nature of this third heaven. I feel like John the Baptist, who trembled when he had to touch the head of Christ in baptism since he knew he was not worthy even to undo his sandal straps. This is how my own soul quivers when I have to begin to speak of this last kind of prayer, and I quake at the prospect of dealing with it. Of course I would not even dare either to give an explanation of this teaching or to aim for such a high spiritual level, if it were not for the goodness, humility, and compassion of Christ, which penetrates all the depths of our misery, giving me the strength and the courage I need. In my heart, as if it were on the highest mountain, my soul enters the embrace of the divinity of Christ, just like Elijah on Mount Carmel, Moses on Mount Sinaï, and the disciples on Mount Tabor. When Christ prayed: 'May they all become one, Father, may they be one in us, as you are in me and I in you' [Jn 17, 21], was it this divine embrace he was asking for? The soul is embraced by Christ's divinity even though it is not changed into that divinity. The soul thus enters into the bosom of the eternal Father and is blessed there in the embraces, the self-giving, and the happiness

that will belong to it through its union with the divine word, which is one with the eternal Father. A simple example may help us best to understand: let us imagine that nobody may embrace the King except his son the Prince. This Prince falls in love with a bleary-eyed vagrant peasant girl and 'wanderer' (*picara*), whom he marries. Holding her tight, he comes with her into the arms of his father the King. The little wanderer now experiences this embrace, she is taken up into that which is taking place between father and son, silent and trembling she herself now has a part in it and assents to what the son asks the father for in her name. She glows in the heart's warmth of the father and the son, and in this mutual giving her own heart is transformed to such a degree that she emerges from their embrace a queen.

Whether in times of sorrow or in times of love, it is characteristic of Father Gracián that his humour never leaves him. But I could not possibly go along with the judgement of many commentators that this demonstrates his superficiality. What I see here is rather a combination of chivalrous nobility with a Christian concern not to take oneself too seriously—something that acquires a particularly attractive tinge where the humour is rooted in a person's nature. Unconditionally committed, Father Gracián was spirited and passionate but never overbearing. In his depiction of the human soul being taken up into the divine Trinitarian life the 'wanderer' is St Teresa: it refers to a famously insulting remark by Nuncio Sega. Objecting to her travelling around making foundations, he labelled her 'a restless vagabond'. Sixteenth century Spain was the cradle of the European picaresque novel, built around the restless wanderings of its protagonists, and Gracián softened the word 'vagabond' to 'wanderer'. Teresa appears 'bleary-eyed' in the portrait that Brother Juan de la Miseria painted of her. Gracián was so impressed by the portrait episode—in which of course he too played a part—that in his later work he came back to it on many occasions. The 'Queen' is Teresa in her posthumous reputation, as the reader will recall from the first chapter.

The *Interior Castle* period, beginning in Toledo and continuing in Avila, brought Teresa a happiness and a stillness not unlike the peaceful eye of the hurricane.

Surrounded

'Outside' meanwhile enemy forces were gathering, encouraged by events which Teresa narrates in the 28th chapter of her Foundations:

> A holy nuncio died who greatly promoted virtue and, as a result, esteemed the discalced. Another nuncio arrived who it seems had been sent by God to test us in suffering. He was a distant relative of the pope, and he must be a servant of God, but he began to take seriously to favouring the calced and in conformity with the information they gave him about us he was convinced that the right thing to do was to put a stop to these foundations. Thus, he began to act with the greatest severity, condemning those he thought could oppose him by imprisoning them or sending them into exile.[10]

Teresa then goes on to report that Father Gracián had inevitably aroused the particular displeasure of the Nuncio. She for her part was hoping that her return to

Toledo would make it possible to allay the troubles—
but it was not to be. Father Gracián continues the story:

> Nuncio Sega came to the Court in Madrid
> claiming to enjoy the same jurisdiction over the
> Orders that he had over the secular clergy. He
> sent to call me, and with many blandishments
> told me I could continue with my office of
> Visitator if I supported his claims. I went to the
> King, … telling him all this and asking him
> what to do … He replied that I should wait until
> he had written to the Pope on this point, for
> without an explicit commission from the Pope
> such as Nuncio Ormaneto had received, I could
> not continue with the visitations…
>
> This meant that on account of the ponderous
> operation of the law, I was caught between the
> King and the Pope. The King's wish was that I
> should not support the Nuncio until an answer
> had come from Rome. The Nuncio was furious
> that I did not stand by him, imputing to me a
> deliberate intent to obstruct the exercise of his
> apostolic jurisdiction. The Pope's message
> however laid down that the Nuncio should not
> interfere with the affairs of the friars except in
> cases where the King was asking him to do so.
> The Nuncio's rage ran so high that he was
> threatening to lay down his office and return to
> Rome if they did not burn me at the stake for
> having obstructed the exercise of his rights. All
> this was aggravated by the slanderous allega-
> tions of the Calced and their demand that I
> ought to be relieved of my office and no longer
> have jurisdiction over them. He was further
> infuriated by memoranda I had presented to
> the King in which I had set out the hugely
> awkward consequences that would ensue in the

religious Orders of Spain, if each Nuncio were permitted to draw up Briefs against the instructions of their Superiors...

I was excommunicated, ...

Worst of all for me was to see our own former Protector, the General of the Order, along with many cardinals writing to the Nuncio to call on him to put an end to the activities of the Discalced and subject them to the Calced: this indeed was just what he proceeded to do. And it was the most agonising of all my sufferings to see the whole Congregation of the Discalced destroyed.

Teresa was still in Toledo when all this happened. In the interests of important administrative reorganisation she moved to St Joseph's Convent in Avila. She therefore had to bring her work on *The Interior Castle* to an end, and it was completed on 29 November.

This was very fortunate, for just four days later came the shocking news that the Calced had taken John of the Cross from the friary in Avila and thrown him into their Order prison in Toledo. Teresa wrote the next day to the King:

... this friar (John of the Cross), who is such a servant of God, is so weak from all his sufferings that I am afraid for his life.

For love of Our Lord, I beseech your Majesty to command that he be set free immediately, and to issue an order, so that all these poor Discalced friars may not have to suffer so much from those of the Cloth. They do nothing but keep silence and suffer, and they gain a great deal by doing so, but the matter is a cause of public scandal...

> Unless Your Majesty orders all this to be reme-
> died, I do not know what will be the end of it
> all, for we have no other remedy upon earth.[11]

But the King could not intervene so quickly and John of the Cross was not able to get out of prison until nine months later, and then only by escaping. Gracián met a similar fate: Nuncio Sega officially subjected the Discalced to the Calced on 16 October 1578, a measure intended to extinguish the Teresian Reform. Gracián was condemned on 20 December to commit himself as prisoner to the Colegio San Cirilo in Alcalá, a founda-tion of the Discalced Carmelites. Earlier he had sought advice and comfort from Mother Teresa. But he did not suffer so badly in Alcalá as John of the Cross in Toledo: '… Fr Elías, who was Rector, loved me very much,' wrote Gracián later in his autobiography, 'and when he was unwell he sometimes appointed me his deputy to stand in for him and lead the chapter; …'

But three friars reported this to the Nuncio, so that things were made very difficult for Father Elías. However, ironically, all of the three accusers died that same summer, and now time, circumstances, and the King began to work generally on behalf of the Dis-calced. Their situation may have seemed utterly hope-less to them, but it was far from being so in God's eyes.

'His is the Victory'

Neither Teresa nor Father Jerónimo Gracián (still less John of the Cross) lost their humility and their compo-sure during these years of persecution and defeat. Their rootedness in God is unmistakable. Gracián always speaks well of his enemies and refuses to attribute to them any bad intentions, only mistakes. Admittedly Teresa—always the more temperamental

one—writes to King Philip that the Calced Carmelites
are even worse than the Moors! But Gracián was adept
at encouraging her. It is instructive to read the following inspirational narrative (which at the same time
demonstrates the very real humility of this man who
called himself arrogant—perhaps a reminder of Teresa's saying: 'There is no worse pride, than when
someone considers himself to be humble!').

Gracián's account runs like this:

> When Nuncio Sega enforced his Brief subjecting
> all the Discalced to the Calced, the alarmed
> superiors of the Discalced gathered in the
> Pastrana friary. In the midst of the delibera-
> tions, ... the Calced brothers ... knocked on the
> priory door. They wanted to read out the Brief
> and call the Discalced to obedience.

Father Gracián was asked for a decision.

> ... I told them to leave me in peace, I said I had
> had more than enough of fighting with the
> Nuncio and all the suffering that went with it,
> let them do what they wanted. They insisted
> that nothing was to be decided unless by my
> order. This plunged me into great confusion
> and distress. Almost all of the Discalced were
> in favour of putting up a fight, while the Calced
> kept on knocking at the door to get us to let
> them in. God be praised that in this priory there
> lived a holy lay brother, Fray Benito de Jesus y
> la Virgen, a man with an awesome reputation.
> So deeply had he identified with his monastic
> calling that he had even forgotten the name of
> his own father: he knew about nothing at all
> other than love for God and Our Lady. He also
> spent a great deal of time praying before the
> most holy sacrament and interceding for the

souls in Purgatory. I believed that God would give me light at such an absolutely crucial juncture by the mouth of this saint, so I went off at once and shut myself up with him in a cell, addressing him as the worthiest, wisest, and most prudent man in the world. I gave him an account of all the circumstances and explained to him the point of view of each party. He started to bang his head on the floor, saying 'I am no good, I am no good' and trying to take refuge in his humility. But I absolutely insisted that he must in God's name tell me his opinion. His answer was:

'Look, my dear fellow, if you go and annoy the small man with the money, the big man with the money gets annoyed and from the black fellow you get absolutely nothing at all. A little while and then a little while, a little grief and then a little more grief, and you will see truly amazing things.'

I listened to these words as if they were those of an angel in heaven, imprinted them on my heart, and translated them to myself thus: if you go and annoy the Nuncio, the Pope will be put out and you will get neither your own Province nor a Brief. Although the King (whom he called the black man because he was a man living in the world) currently favours us and has prohibited the implementation of Sega's Brief, he will eventually abandon us, and basically in the end nothing good will come of it all. To give obedience to the Calced will require a painful struggle which will take time to carry through. Likewise the changes in the rules of the Order and the administrative closure of the monasteries of the Discalced: all a pitiful struggle, but it

will gain time. In the midst of it all new opportunities will open up for negotiation. The main
thing now is not to displease the Nuncio by
declaring his Brief unlawful. If we treat him
well, the Pope will look favourably on us, and
this will help us in our projects.

So I made up my mind and went downstairs
and opened the door to the Calced Masters.
Finding them to be humble and charming
individuals, I told the Discalced to give me the
King's document against Sega's Brief. I kept it
close to my chest and I called the Chapter. The
Calced friars entered and presented their Brief,
I obeyed it submissively and humbly, and the
other Discalced did not dare behave any worse.
I took the Calced friars into the refectory, gave
them something to eat, and asked them to tell
the Nuncio that, although the King had forbidden the presentation of their Brief—and I
showed them the relevant document—nonetheless we Discalced had nothing else in mind but
to obey His Excellency the Nuncio and the most
dear Superiors of the Calced fathers in all
points. So they returned very satisfied, and the
Nuncio had to let go of a good part of his ill will
towards me. From then on everything worked
out very well—as our saintly lay brother had
prophesied.

Thus the prudent Father Gracián did not allow himself
to be crushed between the jurisdictions, but achieved
a master stroke of diplomacy in this game of prestige
between Nuncio, Pope, and King. Actually the Nuncio
was already on the point of changing his mind, partly
because he did not want to spoil things with the King,
and partly because the Calced Carmelites were no
longer his only source of information.

In collaboration with the King, Sega was on the point of going to Pope Gregory XIII (the one who gave his name to our Gregorian Calendar) to obtain an independent province for the Discalced Carmelites. He made one condition however: it must be specifically stated that the Discalced Carmelites were of themselves perfectly reasonable, and that it was only Father Gracián who had stirred them up and misled them. He declared that Gracián's one great offence was his anger, and that if Gracián allowed himself to be sentenced without complaint, everything would be fine for the Discalced and they would be granted their own Province.

'This', said Gracián, 'was the biggest battle of my life'. On the one hand his honour was at stake—and for a Spaniard of noble blood and convictions, honour was the highest good: on the other hand there was the Order, the focus of all his love—and inseparable from his love for Mother Teresa. He took counsel with good theologians, and the advice of the Jesuits was as always especially valuable for him. He concluded that ultimately the Order was the highest good, and that in the matter of honour the fact of his actual innocence mattered far more than what people might think of him. So he sacrificed himself and allowed himself to be condemned and imprisoned in Alcalá.

At this point then the decisive step was taken for the salvation of the Teresian Reform. The Nuncio and the King asked the Pope for a Brief for the Discalced to be granted their own Spanish province. On 1 April 1579 Nuncio Sega revoked his ordinance of October, which had subjected the Discalced to the Calced: 'We desire and ordain that all the Carmelites of Castile and Andalusia who live according to the original rule are to be free from obedience to the Provincials of the mitigated rule and not be subject to them.'

So the Discalced would have their own province, and Gracián took up his office as Provincial again. On 6 June, together with Teresa, he visited Cardinal Quiroga (formerly the Great Inquisitor) in Toledo, and the discussion focussed on the ordinary business of the Order.

On the same day Salazar was appointed the new General of the Order, Rubeo having died. Salazar had been the one to agree to give Teresa permission for her first foundation, so for her his appointment amounted to a starter's gun! She visited her convents in Toledo, Valladolid, Alba de Tormes, Medina del Campo, Salamanca, and Malagón. And on 28 January 1580 General Salazar sent her a new foundation patent. But the Mother of the Order was still waiting impatiently for the Brief of Separation.

This was eventually issued by Pope Gregory XIII on 22 June 1580. In its very first sentence it stated that the Discalced should be freed through this Bull and this Brief from all pressures, in conformity with the special request of 'Our beloved son in Christ King Philip II'. The Pope then gave a concise survey of the history of the Order and declared that: 'about the year 1565 a few friars, (!) moved by God's grace, wanted to follow the original Rule again in all its severity. So with the permission of the Prior General in the Kingdom of Spain they began to found monasteries for monks and nuns.' The Pope gives precise figures: up to this point 22 houses founded with a total of 300 monks and 200 nuns in them. In complete contrast with today, the men were in the majority at that time, which further underlined the importance of Gracián's role.

To begin with, the Bull listed the features of the original rule which would be reintroduced in the Teresian convents: abstention from meat and shared seclusion (enclosure), in order 'to immerse themselves day and night in God's law in the cells.' (The official Carmelite translation of the Rule of Albert runs today: 'Each one of you is to stay in his own cell or nearby, pondering the Lord's law day and night and keeping watch at his prayers'.)

The Pope goes on to give the new additional regulations: no shoes (sandals not being regarded as shoes), clothing of coarse cloth, sleeping on boards, manual labour, frequent exercise of interior prayer, and in worship simple recitation in a monotone. (These may look like trivial details, but for Teresa it was all about the spirit to which such details gave expression.)

Admittedly the Pope still kept the Discalced subject to the (reasonable) Calced Order General, Salazar, so they were not yet an independent Order. But they retained a relative independence that was very important in practice, in that they were to choose a Provincial for all the foundations in Spain out of their own ranks. He would retain wide-ranging rights: 'To lead and govern the separated Province, to reform, to correct, and (when necessary) to punish. He may make and change, found and erect monasteries wherever it seems good to him, without needing to get any other approval than the fundamental assent of the above-mentioned Chapter of the Province.

He may also in the future call Chapter meetings and delegate further duties. 'He has, like all monks of this Province, free access to the Holy See. The Province especially set up by us will be called that of the 'Discalced'. The monks of the mitigated Rule (the

'Calced') have moreover no longer any right to molest, trouble, disturb, or ill-treat the Discalced.'

In order that peace might be complete, the Pope lifted all excommunications and Church punishments that had been imposed, including those applying to Teresa and Gracián! He put this all very clearly: 'With this document we free all Discalced monks and nuns from excommunications and other ecclesiastical punishments, whenever and for whatever reason they were imposed. We declare our absolution. The content of this writing is to be made known everywhere.' (It is largely unknown today.)

On 20 November of the same year Pope Gregory went on to write to the Dominican Prior Juan de las Cuevas at Toledo: he was to call the Provincial Chapter together 'as soon as possible', with the new independent status of the Discalced and the choice of their Provincial and further office-bearers on the agenda. The neutral Dominican set up the Chapter at the beginning of March 1581 and chose as venue for the meeting the College in Alcalá where Gracián had been held under arrest shortly before.

On 24 January 1581 King Philip II wrote to the Dominican Prior:

> I welcome the intention of having the Chapter meet in Alcalá de Henares, and I find your reasons for that quite convincing. So that you can obtain the details and the information you will need, I ask you to make contact with the Discalced Carmelite Father Gracián, who is currently administering the affairs of the Order. He knows about everything, from the first foundations onward, and he is so learned and so concerned for the wellbeing of the Order that you can trust him absolutely and make use of

his advice now and in the future. The Bishop of Piacenza and Nuncio of his Holiness (Sega) is here in Madrid today and he has been applying himself zealously to the whole business. He knows the papal bull (for the separation), which you now have in your hands. I have also informed the Rector of the University of Alcalá of your forthcoming visit and prepared him for it so that he can be helpful to you. I would be delighted if you would keep me informed about developments.

–I, the King.

On 4 March of the same year this then was the progress made so far, and Teresa was delighted:

While I was in Palencia, God willed that the discalced Carmelites be separated from the calced. This was done by letting the discalced form their own province, which was all that we were desiring for the sake of our peace and tranquillity. At the request of our Catholic king, Don Philip, a very long brief was obtained from Rome for this purpose (Bull Pope Gregory XIII, 22 June 1580)…the chapter was held in the College of St Cyril, that of our discalced friars. They elected Father Maestro Gracián de la Madre de Dios as provincial…

… And this for me was one of the great joys and satisfactions of my life. It would take a long time to tell of the trials, persecutions, and afflictions that I have had to undergo during the past twenty-five years, and only our Lord can understand them. Save for anyone who knows the trials that were suffered, one cannot grasp the joy that came to my heart at seeing the matter concluded and the desire I had that everyone

> praise our Lord and that we pray for this our
> holy king, Don Philip. By means of him God
> brought the matter to a happy ending. Had it
> not been for the king, the devil was so cunning
> that everything would have collapsed.
>
> Now we are all at peace, Calced and Discalced;
> no one can hinder us from serving our Lord.
> Hence, my Brothers and Sisters, since His
> Majesty has heard your prayers so well, let us
> make haste to serve Him.[12]

The statutes worked out by Gracián (Expositions of the Rule of the Order) were accepted. Teresa saw her vision of 1575 confirmed: 'His is the victory'. She was happy. Her closest friends were not entirely happy however, for neither the Pope nor the Nuncio had mentioned Teresa or her founding activity in their documents. The Chapter met completely apart from her. Prioress Maria de San José complained: 'Not a word is said about our Mother, still less about her foundations for nuns and friars. So it could happen that at some difficult time in the future, those who did not know better would attribute this honour to themselves.'

On this subject 'Cirilo' said:

> Her right to this title, the authority she held
> from the General of the Order which designated
> her as 'Foundress', and the number of monas-
> teries she founded, is something I want to talk
> to you about another time, Eliseo. At the
> moment I simply cannot endure for people to
> do her an injustice and cast doubt on her right
> to the title of Foundress and attempt to diminish
> her eternal fame, since she brought such new
> and valuable things into this world.

Then Cirilo, an extremely knowledgeable man, went through the famous women of Antiquity, whose inventions extended from the spindle to the working of gold to the extraction of olive oil, and then opined: 'How much more right has the Mother foundress to eternal fame, since she called into life monasteries in which the Holy Ghost will be served for ever, monasteries whose worship is pleasing to our Lord and glorifies Him?'

Gracián very sensitively prefaced his statutes for the nuns with a letter to the holy Mother, the only one to Teresa in his hand that has survived:

> To the most reverend Mother Teresa of Jesus, foundress of the monasteries of Discalced Carmelites.
>
> HE, true light of all who come into this world, HE, who hides all the treasures of wisdom and knowledge in his divine heart, does not refuse the brightness of the highest knowledge to women. Rather he enlightens them so that they attain to Christian perfection and shine as stars in the heavenly vault of the Catholic Church.
>
> Our divine Lord, who would like to lead all to salvation and to knowledge of the truth, has then, as I know, chosen your Reverence to impart the true light to your daughters in the monasteries of the Discalced Carmelites founded by you. HE has provided you, Reverend Mother, with an abundance of spirituality and knowledge, prudence and tact, wit and practical sense, on top of your fifty years of experience of the spiritual life. As a result of this, and moreover through your contact with the best theologians and spiritual directors of our day, to whom your reverence was always

obedient, you have been gifted with such salu-
tary counsels and exhortations for your daughters, that under your leadership they will attain
to the Christian perfection which they yearn for.
Your Reverence strives for them to attain it, and
I as your Superior am sworn to demand it.

All this was a cause of great joy, and the high degree
of mutual understanding bore an abundance of fruit.
Father Silverio de Santa Teresa characterised the
situation in this way:

> If the small vessel of the Discalced reached safe
> harbour without a shipwreck, nobody deserves
> gratitude for this as much as Mother Teresa
> except Father Gracián de la Madre de Dios, who
> quite rightly holds the title 'Father of the Reform'
> by reason of his heroic and victorious struggles
> on behalf of the Order. Apart from Father John
> of the Cross, I know nobody who had such a
> claim to this title of honour, he should never
> have been robbed of it by ingratitude. If Provi-
> dence then allowed him to be overwhelmed by
> the waves of the dark sea of suffering and
> persecution, we ought to reflect that a Jonah is
> often necessary in order to save the other ship-
> wrecked crew. When the storms engulfing the
> Reform reached hurricane strength, you could
> always see Mother Teresa and Father Gracián on
> the bridge, firmly resolved either to win out or
> go down together.

Notes

1   *Foundations* ch. 27, xx in *CW* iii, 248.
2   'Teresa uses the term 'accidental joy' in the theological sense
    of her time, but with a very original application. Accidental joy
    was that joy experienced by the blessed in heaven that did not
    flow directly from their vision of God.' [Footnote at *CW* iii, 435.]

3   *Foundations* ch. 27, xx in *CW* iii, 249.

4   *Letters* I, 358, no 141 Nov 1576)

5   *Letters* I, 257 no 101, 24 July 1576.

6   *Letters* I, 263 no 103, Aug 1576.

7   *Foundations* 45/46 in *CW* iii, 351.

8   *The Interior Castle* 1:1, i/iii in *CW* ii, 283.

9   *The Interior Castle* VII:1 in *CW* ii, 430.

10 *Foundations* ch. 28, iii in *CW* iii, 251.

11 *Letters* I, 497 no 204, 4 Dec 1577.

12 *Foundations* ch. 29, xxx/xxxi in *CW* iii, 278.

6

TODAY THERE IS A FULL MOON

Winding Paths

THE HAPPINESS THEY had experienced in Alcalá proved to be as changeable as the waxing and waning moon. Already in May Teresa was writing to Gracián: 'Now do you not see how short-lived my happiness has been? I was looking forward to the journey … So I must remind you, my Father, that, after all, the flesh is weak, and what has happened has made me sadder than I could have wished to be: it has been a great blow to me.'[1]

What had happened? Teresa wanted to found a convent in Soria. In the previous year Gracián had stood by her side at the founding of Palencia. Now however he had delegated another priest to travel with the saint. This was his commission: 'I herewith charge Prior Fray Nicolás de Jesús María to proceed to Palencia to Mother Teresa de Jesús and to accompany her to Soria for the foundation of a convent of nuns in the said town.'

So what had happened, and who was this priest? Genoese by birth, as talented as Gracián, he had entered the Order at the age of forty in 1577 after a turbulent life. Teresa knew him already as a man of the world, for he was a financial genius and so versed in every kind of intrigue that the biographer of the Order Father Silverio labelled him 'Machiavellian'. His civil name was Nicolás Doria. He also had another side to his character: a strong mystical gift and above all—in reaction to his earlier 'high life'—an ascetical bent which increasingly expressed itself in a strangely Old Testament-style type of severe legalism. After a long search his choice of vocation had fallen on Teresa's Order, which he had already been advising in financial matters.

Several of her letters show that Teresa was therefore very keen to get to know him. Her wish was finally fulfilled in the year 1579. She wrote to her friend Maria de San José on 24 June: 'You must know that Father Nicolas is here; he is now Prior of Pastrana. He came to see me and gave me a very great deal of comfort, and I praised Our Lord for having given the Order a person like that—so full of virtue.'[2]

Naturally Teresa soon started to ponder how the gifted Doria would best fit in. On 7 July she wrote to Father Gracián, not aware (or perhaps she was) that from now on a new chapter in the life and history of the Order was to be opened:

> Father Nicolas spent three or four days with me in Avila. It was a great comfort to me to know that your Paternity has someone now to discuss matters concerning the Order with, someone who can help you in a way that gives me great satisfaction. It has worried me dreadfully to see you quite alone in the Order, as you have been. I thought him really sensible, and a good person to go to for advice, and a servant of God, though he does not have the graciousness and serenity that God has given to Paul—there are very few to whom He has given so many gifts at once as He has to him. But Father Nicolas is certainly a sound man, full of humility and penitence, with a great regard for truth and able to win others'

good will. He will fully recognize how valuable
Paul is and he is quite resolved to follow him
in everything, and I was very glad to see that.
In many respects, if Paul gets on well with
him — and I believe he will, if only to please
me — it will be very advantageous for them both
to be of one mind, and it will be the greatest
relief... So your Paternity must not be distant
with him, for, unless I am very much mistaken,
he will be a great help in many ways.[3]

Subsequent events may seem to set a question mark
against this judgement, and Gracián was certainly to
suffer grievously for it, but nonetheless Nicolas Doria
had indeed given evidence of his unusual diplomatic
capacities immediately following his entry into the
Order. He was sent to Madrid, where he had to stay
with the Calced friars. They did not take the novice
seriously, and so he was able to work out of their
priory like the proverbial Trojan horse. The change of
mind on the part of Nuncio Sega, the efforts of the King
with the Pope, the freeing of the illustrious prisoners
of the Order, and the Bull of separation all had their
origin in Doria's secret activities in Rome. No wonder
Teresa wanted to see this deserving man in an influ-
ential position. But her instinct? Her instinct was
against going with Doria to Soria!

Yet she again called on Gracián to collaborate with
Doria in the preparation of the Chapter of the Order
at Alcalá: 'Another thing that has occurred to me is
this. If your Reverence is elected Provincial, you
should see that you have Father Nicolao as your
companion, for in these early stages it will be very
important for you to have someone to accompany you.'[4]

This was exactly what the Chapter then decided,
and Gracián seemed at first to be in agreement. But

soon he kept on finding new tasks for Doria, tasks which took the latter away from him, until eventually he sent him as a kind of ambassador of the Order to the General in Rome. Today it is difficult to assess Gracián's motivation here: was he acting out of some secret aversion arising from a mutual irreconcilability of their dispositions, or was he actually convinced that there really was nobody better qualified for this task than Doria? Members of the Order—and indeed Teresa herself—felt that an aversion on Gracián's part was involved and they were annoyed.

Gracián's childlike and loving heart felt their reproaches bitterly. Up to now Teresa herself had basically been guiding the Order through him: he was her '*Socio*'. Since Doria's intervention, everything had been different (and often far from pleasing to Teresa, something that had come home to her with Gracián's behaviour over Doria-Soria!).

Yet while Doria later actively undermined Gracián in every possible way, even to the point of calling for his dismissal at the Order Chapter of 1583 just after Teresa's death, Gracián never spoke ill of Doria, and indeed even 'thanked' him for all his later misfortune in life. His real feelings emerge only indirectly. He explained his conception of the monastic life and the administration of the Order in a later Apologia:

> It is true that I incline more to mildness than to severity, more to love than to hatred, more to peace than to anger, and that I prefer to do good to others rather than evil. Also I was always of the opinion that I should not be infringing right and conscience if I remitted a punishment. Moreover, if an Order grows in numbers and confidence because it is led in peace with love,

> there is no reason to turn the page and resort to
> severity and harshness. Finally the superiors of
> the order are 'fathers' and not official judges or
> slave overseers. And the friars, those servants
> of God and sons of honourable parents, are
> neither slaves nor *Picaros* (unscrupulous vaga-
> bonds).

Here a Perceval, a pure gateway to the grail and a
guardian of it[5], is confronted with an alien spirit,
someone who appears inhuman to him, someone he
cannot follow. Teresa saw this, understood it, and
suffered. Her prophetic spirit sensed in advance the
difficulties that would overwhelm Father Gracián in
the Order, but her warnings were so many words
spoken into the wind. The coming tragedy cast
shadows over this love, and their original mutual
understanding lost its power, even if their personal
friendship endured unspoiled, springing as it did from
deeper sources.

With Aelred of Rivaulx, who sang to the Middle
Ages the song of spiritual friendship, we could say:

> … love is the source of friendship, not love of
> any sort whatever, but that which proceeds from
> reason and affection simultaneously, which,
> indeed, is pure because of reason and sweet
> because of affection… a foundation of friendship
> should be laid in the love of God, to which all
> things which are proposed should be referred,
> and these ought to be examined as to whether
> they conform to the foundation or are at variance
> with it.

But not every 'neighbour' is also our friend: 'We love
many persons, but it would be ill-considered if we
exposed our souls and opened up our hearts to all of

them, for not every other person, not everyone's mind or capacity for judgement is mature enough to bear this.'

Thus Teresa could recommend collaboration with Doria to her friend Father Jerónimo while at the same time complaining when she had to go with Doria instead of with Gracián on foundation travels. In the letter of 22 May 1581 she wrote:

> I have been very lonely here: ...
>
> I cannot really write anything properly now, and have very little desire to do so...
>
> Everything will be distasteful to me now, for, after all, the soul feels the absence of one who both governs it and brings it relief. May all this conduce to God's service; and if that happens, however much we suffer, we have no cause for complaint.[6]
>
> Oh, my Father, praise God for granting you the gift of getting on so well with people you meet that no one seems able to take your place. Oh, how tired poor Laurencia is of everything! She commends herself earnestly to your Reverence, and says her soul can find no peace or quiet in anyone but God, and in those who understand her, as your Reverence does. Everything else is such a cross to her that no one can adequately describe it.[7]

Gracián did actually go with her on her travels again—now though more as friend and companion, a lovable protector and anxious father for the ailing, tired, but tireless foundress. Madrid was a possibility they discussed, then Granada or Burgos. Teresa, who had never had any love for Andalusia, decided to leave the founding of Granada to the gifted although hugely individualistic Prioress Ana de Jesus. She made this decision at the last moment, when John of the Cross was already there (here was a person of quite a different stamp, greater though inwardly different) to fetch her. Teresa refused and said 'Burgos!' She also said 'Father Jerónimo', to whom she wrote: 'You should know I have no one to go with, so do not think of leaving me in the cold.'[8]

When Teresa wrote 'leaving me in the cold', it was of course meant metaphorically, but it also applied literally to the hard winter journey to Burgos. At this point Teresa was once more Prioress of St Joseph in Avila. She had resisted this charge with all her might and implored Father Gracián to release her from it, for she felt she needed to use the time that might still be left to her wholly for God. With hindsight Gracián thought that she sensed the nearness of her end. But things were so bad in the Avila Convent—Teresa wrote 'they chose me out of pure hunger'—that an experienced leader was urgently needed. 'With the greatest charm in the world' Teresa had set out to explain her reasons for wanting to refuse the appointment to the assembly, but Father Gracián had simply commanded her to kneel down with her face on the floor while he struck up a joyful *Te Deum* with the nuns. Teresa got up blushing and smiling happily. To make the office easier for her, Gracián had introduced a vote for a sub-prioress, so Teresa was able to delegate a great deal.

Now the journey to Burgos had become possible. Gracián met Teresa on 24 January in Palencia. Just two days later they reached Burgos—an achievement that would do honour to any winter sportsman, writes a biographer. This journey through deep snow, to the accompaniment of squalls of rain and floods, was to be the last one they took together. Teresa reported:

> Father Provincial wanted to accompany us on this foundation. He did so partly because he was unoccupied at the time, ... and partly because he wanted to look after my health on the journey, for the weather was harsh, and I, old and sick; and they think my life is somewhat important. Certainly this was the Providence of God, for the roads were so flooded from the heavy rains that he and his companions were very necessary to guide us along the way and help pull the wagons out of the mire. This was especially so on the trip from Palencia to Burgos, which was a very daring one to make at that time. True, our Lord told me that we could go without harm, that I should not fear, that He would be with us; although I did not tell this then to Father Provincial. But these words consoled me in the great hardships and dangers that we were going through. There was special danger in a river crossing near Burgos called Paso de los Pontones. The rain had been so heavy and had lasted so long that the water flooded the bridge. As a result, the bridge could not be seen nor could we see where to pass, but all was water, and everywhere it was very deep. In sum, it was a great imprudence to cross there, especially with wagons, for just by veering a little from the course all would have been lost. In fact, one of the wagons did get into a dangerous situation.[9]

In his report Gracián added: 'When a wagon almost came off the bridge, Our Dear Lady appeared to the Mother and said to her: 'Do not be afraid, I am with you.' So the Mother carried on cheerfully and calmly while we others were trembling for fear and covered with mud.'

Gracián experienced a moment of great fear on this journey—almost a premonition: a coachman fell from the wagon and was a hairsbreadth away from slipping under the wheels. For a moment, mistaking the mud-covered edge of his cloak for *alpargatas* (hemp sandals), Gracián actually thought it was Mother Teresa herself lying there: 'I was momentarily paralysed by fear and on the point of falling off my mule in a faint, but then I pulled myself together and spurred him on to get quickly to the wagon. There I saw that the young man who had fallen under it had got up again at once and I found everyone alive and well.'

Teresa's health would in fact have quite rightly been a cause for concern, for she was actually struggling at the time with the pain of an advanced cancer, though the presence of the cancer could not have been known about then. Yet her habitual composure and kindness were very much in evidence on this journey. What ultimately mattered more than anything to her was not the letter of the Rule of her own Order but God-given love in the heart, and she was therefore more attracted to Gracián than to Doria: this was demonstrated in a little scene which so impressed Father Jerónimo that he reported it in detail. With Gracián's permission, a nobleman who had done something for the Order and who had a great love for Teresa, approached the wagon in which Teresa sat with Gracián unveiled. When she realised that a stranger wanted to see her, she drew her veil over her face in fright. Yet when Father Jerónimo explained to her who it was, she pulled the veil back again and bent out of the wagon and embraced the happy man, whose cheeks ran with tears of joy.

The foundation in Burgos took three months on account of all the various involvements with the spiritual authorities, but it proved to be just as eventful as the journey to get there had been. Not until 18 April could the monastery be consecrated through Holy Mass. Gracián's friends were very helpful throughout this period. It was a time when he himself came and went as his office required, but now Teresa felt more relaxed in his absence—she preferred not to see him embroiled in all the troublesome and irritating episodes involved in the process of this foundation.

When it was all over she felt totally exhausted. Gracián ordered her to return to Avila in order to rest in the convent there. He himself could not accompany her in spite of her request for him to do so, because a difficulty had arisen in Beas—of which Gracián spoke later. Someone had played a foolish trick on the nuns there for their Recreation (their evening period of relaxation together), which involved convincing them that they must spend it saying 'I believe in God, I love God etc.' as they counted on their fingers. Some felt they were robbed thereby of the proper relaxation, and the Provincial Vicar, whom Gracián had sent as his representative to Andalusia, prohibited the game. This rather drastic measure was imprudent, for now the nuns got scruples and reported to their confessors that they were not supposed to say that they believed in God, loved him, etc. Some of the confessors were quite appalled by this and they immediately reported to the Inquisition that in the Order of the Discalced Carmelites it was forbidden to believe in God and love him etc. Gracián, whose representative had lost control of the situation, had therefore to go off 'to put out the fire in Beas'.

I had a bad night

Teresa went on through Palencia to Valladolid. The days that followed in the convent there proved to be among the darkest of her entire life. Recalcitrant prioresses had been opposing her ever-increasingly since she had grown old and sick, but what happened to her in Valladolid seems almost beyond belief. The cause of it was her involvement in an inheritance battle in her family in which the Avila convent was at stake. Teresa, who wanted to keep the convent independent, saw herself suddenly quite alone, betrayed even by her little nieces from Peru whom she always had with her. The Prioress of Valladolid, her trusted friend and cousin, strongly opposed her view, to the point where in the end she actually threw Teresa out. Ana de San Bartolomé tells the story: 'On this occasion she (Prioress Maria Bautista) demonstrated a huge lack of respect. She told us we must go with God and leave her house. And as we were leaving she actually shoved me out of the door with the words: 'Get out, both of you and don't be seen here ever again!'

Still in Valladolid, Teresa wrote the bitterest of letters to Father Gracián. It was also her last. Her desolation was unmistakable and she manifested an acute anxiety about the future of her friend and of her Order. She set out in her customary manner to provide a report of her doings and to tell the story, but something nameless seems to be have been broken. Teresa was quite alone:

> May the grace of the Holy Spirit be with your Reverence. Your frequent letters to me do not

suffice to alleviate my distress, though it was a great relief to me to know you are well and the south is free from sickness. God grant this may continue. As far as I know I have had all your letters.

The reasons you gave for your decision to go did not seem to me sufficient, ...

So keenly did I feel your being away at such a time that I lost the desire to write to you: so I have not written till today, when it is unavoidable. Today is full moon: I had a perfectly wretched night and my head is bad this morning. Until now I had been better, and tomorrow, when the moon is past the full, I think this indisposition will disappear. The throat trouble is better, but has not yet gone...

I cannot think how your Reverence did not realize that ... this is no time to found a house in Rome, for your Reverence is very short of men even for the houses here. Also you badly need Nicolas, for I don't think you can possibly attend to so many things at once. Fray Juan de las Cuevas (the Dominican president of the Provincial chapter of Alcalá) made that remark to me and I had several conversations with him (about the matter). He is very anxious that your Reverence should be successful in all you do and I am under a great debt to him for his affection for you. He even said to me that your Reverence was acting contrarily to the ordinances, which laid it down that, when the Provincial had no coadjutor, a fresh one should be elected — I am not sure if he said this needed the consent of the Priors. He also said he considered it impossible for you to manage alone: Moses, he said, had any number of people to help him. I told him there was no one suitable, and we could not even find enough priors. He said that was more important than anything else...

Be careful about this, for the love of God, and also about preaching down there in Andalusia. I never like it when your Reverence is down there for long. You wrote to me the other day about the trials people have been suffering there: (I pray that) God will not give me the grief of seeing you in the same plight. As your Reverence says, the devil never slumbers. At any rate, you may be sure I shall feel dreadfully worried as long as you are there.

I do not know what purpose your Reverence can have in staying for so long at Seville. I am told you will not come (north) before the Chapter, and that news greatly increases my distress—it is even worse than if you returned to Granada. May the Lord guide you to do what is most conducive to His service. There is very great need for a vicar there. If Fray Antonio does well here, your Reverence might seriously consider giving him that office. Do not meditate turning yourself into an Andalusian: you are not of a temperament to live among them. As for your sermons there, I earnestly beg your Reverence once again to be very careful what you say, even though you preach but rarely...

The letter I wrote to the community at Alba (de Tormes) saying how annoyed with them I was, and that I shall certainly pay them a visit, has been very effective. All will be well there... Oh, my Father, how oppressed I have been feeling lately! But the oppression passed off when I

> heard you were well. May God be pleased to
> prosper you henceforward.
>
> Give my remembrances to the Mother Prioress
> and all the sisters. I am not writing to them, as
> they will get news of me from this letter. I was
> glad to hear they are well and I earnestly beg
> them not to wear your Reverence out, but to
> look after you. My kind regards to Father Fray
> John of the Cross. San Bartolomé sends your
> Reverence her remembrances. May Our Lord
> watch over you, as I beseech Him to, and
> deliver you from all dangers. Amen.[10]

The letter illustrates Teresa's concern both for the
future of the Order and for the future role in it of Father
Gracián—which she defended against the Dominican.
But it also shows her personal suffering over Gracián's
absence, which did not seem absolutely necessary to
her, so that it felt very much like a lack of love,
friendship, and support.

Along with the complaints about not writing
enough that are part of the 'stock in trade' of this
exchange of letters, fresh lamentations appeared about
his frequent absences—which of course were in some
cases far from being Gracián's fault. For example
Teresa wrote to him when he was under house arrest
in Alcalá: 'God keep you, for if anything could give
me any pleasure, it would be to see Paul. But if it is not
God's will that I should, may His will be done: let Him
send me one cross upon another.'[11]

It is of course part and parcel of the *Unio mystica*
that it erects its cross on the ground of love. I rather
doubt however whether Father Gracián would quite
have been able to comprehend these complaints
addressed to him—which would have been uncom-

fortable to any man. I say this not because I consider him, as does Father Silverio, who was very favourably disposed towards him, 'to be a person who loved everyone and no one'. He was very well aware of the uniqueness of this friendship and of the irreplaceable preciousness of his holy Mother Saint Teresa of Jesus. Everything he said testifies to that. But as her confessor with a responsibility for her, and indeed as a much younger man with so much less experience of life, he was inclined to look with a certain mistrust on her all-too-unconcealed expressions of love and yearning.

Of course he was not used to dealing with nuns living in union with God, nuns whose love was therefore assuredly one with God's love. Hence he later has Anastasio say:

> As a (womanly) soul loves Christ interiorly, so her love for her father confessor will show itself outwardly too. But it seems as if this love for Christ and for her father confessor slides into the sensual, and since the devil is not inactive, the result is that one or both of them want to see and converse with the other constantly and to be in a relationship. Then one is tormented by the illnesses or absence of the other, by his sufferings, and by the adequacy or inadequacy of the signs of love that are given. Jealousy comes onto the scene, though it is often decked out as something spiritual: does the father confessor recommend her soul to God the same as he does others? Does he devote enough time to her inner problems? etc...

In this connection Eliseo describes how a nun had a vision of Mother Teresa warning her that for all her strong belief about the chaste life led by Mary and

Joseph together, she herself must still keep clear of all
intimacy with her confessor.

We can glimpse here only a little of what was going
on in the soul of Father Jerónimo when he felt he must
absent himself for a while for the sake of the wellbeing
of his holy penitent Mother Teresa. But in any case he
was quite simply overloaded with a whole multitude
of tasks in the Order. Moreover he must also have been
'once bitten, twice shy' after being the object of so
many persecutions and slanders which hit him harder
than anyone, even though Teresa herself was affected
by them too.

Above all he had absolutely no idea at the time that
in actual fact what Teresa was begging him for was his
company on what was to be her last journey. He had
seen her ill and under ever-increasing strain all too
often before. Moreover he could hardly have known
that she would simply be unable to implement his
directive to go back to Avila to rest.

For one thing, she found it difficult to rest because
it was in her nature to keep a close eye on things, and
the last letter shows that in Alba they were already
jittery that she might be coming there. For another
thing, because of Gracián's long stay in Andalusia, it
was now his Vicar Fr Antonio de Jesus who was
making the decisions. Even before Teresa left Valladolid on 15 September, a letter from him had arrived
telling her not to go to Avila but to Alba de Tormes
instead—less because there was a Prioress to be elected
there, than because a grandchild was about to be born
to the illustrious Countess of Alba. This lady wanted
Teresa to be in the neighbourhood for the confine-
ment—a silly reason but one which, on grounds of
diplomacy and obedience, Teresa could not oppose.

She remarked however—as her niece related—that obedience had never in her whole life been so burdensome to her as on this occasion.

Teresa made her way through Medina del Campo and arrived in Alba de Tormes on 20 September. Meanwhile the child in question had come into the world prematurely. When the saint arrived she felt totally exhausted: completely against her normal practice, she took herself straight off to bed. On the next day she struggled out of bed with the greatest difficulty to get to Holy Communion. Her condition quickly worsened. Weakness owing to severe haemorrhages was intensified by the bleeding that was customary then—it was the universal cure-all for the medicine of the day. Even though her condition strongly suggested that the end was near, Teresa continued to receive visits from persons plaguing her with monastic, financial, and foundation matters—and those anything but pleasant.

On the morning of 3 October she received the sacrament of the dying. She recommended to the weeping nuns that they keep the Rule and the Statutes of the Order rather better than she had done herself. Many 'last words' of hers have been handed down, and many seem all too appropriate. It is certain that in these her last days Teresa repeated again and again the Latin verse of the Psalm *'Cor contritum et humiliatum, Deus, non despicies'* (the *Miserere*). Father Gracián had taught her to pray Latin verses. In English: 'A humbled, contrite heart you will not spurn' (Ps 50, 19).

Teresa had emptied her cup of suffering to the very bottom. On the morning of 4 October she lay down on her side and seemed lost in prayer. She looked very happy. At around nine o'clock that night her heart, which had lived nothing but love, stopped beating.

It was the night in which the Catholic world introduced the Gregorian Calendar, the night of the 4 to 15 October. It is as though time ceased to be in force on this night, making space for a breakthrough of eternity.

It does not fall within the scope of this book to tell of the miracles at and after the death of St Teresa of Jesus, but a few words are in order on the subject of her inner being, her 'soul', where this final departure had long been prepared for. Did Gracián know her last *'Cuenta de Conciencia'*? This report of inner experience from May 1581, written in Palencia around the time when he sent her on the journey with Doria, was addressed to the Bishop of Osma, her previous confessor. Teresa had already attained to detachment, as she showed in her deeply human and moving letters. A better way of putting this would be to say that knowing how to enjoy human attachments while not being tied down by them were for her entirely compatible aspirations. She could have felt the love of God with Gracián near her, but God decreed that she should be alone. In these final moments she showed that she was still moving forward in the spiritual life.

In *the Interior Castle* she had described the condition of *Unio mystica*:

> It seems that I am saying that when the soul reaches this state in which God grants it this favour, it is sure of its salvation and safe from falling again. I do not say such a thing, and wherever I so speak that it seems the soul is secure, this should be taken to mean as long as the Divine Majesty keeps it in His hand and it does not offend Him. At least I know certainly

that the soul doesn't consider itself safe even
though it sees itself in this state and the state
has lasted for some years. But it goes about with
much greater fear than before, guarding itself
from any small offence against God and with
the strongest desires to serve Him, as will be
said further on, and with habitual pain and
confusion at seeing the little it can do and the
great deal to which it is obliged. The pain is no
small cross but a very great penance.[12]

Now, four years on, Teresa wrote:

Oh, who would be able to explain to your
Excellency the quiet, and calm my soul experiences! It is so certain it will enjoy God that it
thinks it already enjoys the possession of Him,
although not the fruition…

… to put it truthfully, this soul is no longer in
part subject to the miseries of the world as it
used to be. For although it suffers more, this is
only on the surface. The soul is like a lord in his
castle, and so it doesn't lose its peace; although
this security doesn't remove a great fear of
offending God and of not getting rid of all that
would be a hindrance to serving Him. The soul
rather proceeds more cautiously, but it goes
about so forgetful of self that it thinks it has
partly lost its being. In this state everything is
directed to the honour of God, to the greater
fulfilment of His will, and to His glory…

… the soul has well understood that His
Majesty knows what is fitting for the accomplishment of this, and it is so withdrawn from
self-interest, these desires and acts come to an
end quickly, and in my opinion they don't have
any force…

The imaginative visions have ceased, but it seems this intellectual vision of these three Persons and of the humanity of Christ always continues...

It seems I live only to eat and sleep and not suffer in anything; and even this does not bother me, although sometimes, as I say, I fear lest I be deceived. But I'm not able to believe that I am, because from all that I can discern there doesn't reign in me any strong attachment to any creature or to all the glory of heaven, but rather to loving this God of ours. This attachment to loving God doesn't diminish; instead, in my opinion, it increases along with the desire that all serve Him.

But besides the love, one thing amazes me: that those interior feelings that were so extreme and used to torment me, when I saw souls being lost and I thought about whether some offence was committed against God, cannot be felt by me any longer; although I don't think the desire that He not be offended is any less...

And, as a result I no longer have any need to seek out learned men or tell any one anything. I only need the satisfaction of knowing ...

The presence of the three Persons is ... impossible to doubt ...

This presence is almost continual, except when a lot of sickness weighs down on one. For it sometimes seems God wants one to suffer without interior consolation; but never, not even in its first stirrings, does the will turn from its desire that God's will be done in it.

This surrender to the will of God is so powerful that the soul wants neither death nor life, unless for a short time when it longs to die to see God. But soon the presence of the Three Persons is represented to it so forcefully that this presence provides a remedy for the pain caused by His absence, and there remains the desire to live, if He wills, in order to serve Him more. And if through my intercession I could play a part in getting a soul to love and praise God more, even if it be for just a short time, I think that would matter more to me than being in glory.[13]

Eliseo receives some news

The circle was complete: the news of Teresa's death reached Gracián on 22 October in Beas, where they had met for the first time. He recorded his reaction in a distressing document. He later referred to this in the last chapter of his autobiography as 'Dialogue between Angela and Eliseo'. I found the notes 'hidden' in a periodical.[14] But they look more like a diary entry than a dialogue. Gracián does not succeed in keeping the 'Eliseo' fiction going fully. In his emotion he sometimes falls back into using the first person. I quote the document with small abridgements:

> At four o'clock in the afternoon, Eliseo received the news that Angela had entered into God's eternity. The suddenness and harshness of this blow, the worst of his whole life, a blow which he had always feared, sent him into a kind of traumatic state. He was numb, he felt coldness in all his limbs, his whole body trembled. At first he just wanted to throw himself onto his bed, but then he realised he did not have the courage to be alone, for his grief threatened to

overwhelm him completely. He knew he must
not allow that to happen, for it would distress
and trouble Christ, the Holy Bridegroom, and
His Mother, Our dear Lady, and sadden his
Angela. In the end he did what he had always
done when struggling under similar blows of
fate, he took refuge with the Most Holy Sacrament, where he could always find and love the
one who in His infinite goodness gives boundless comfort.

In this presence and this love his soul found
rest, although the shaking and the coldness in
his limbs persisted. A feeling of loneliness sank
into him like an inner mist, an oppressive
weight even more painful than the growing
outer suffering and anxiety that tormented him
because of the loss of Angela. He remained lost
like this in comfortless sadness for many hours,
not daring to leave the place of the holy presence and prayer, unable to see how to cope with
the heaviness of his feelings.

He did not dare to come out because he was
afraid that the Sisters, seeing what a state he
was in, would question him, and he simply did
not have the courage to be the bearer of such
tragic news to them. After a while he was able
to speak to his divine Mother. The conversation
was as ever both deeply earnest and gentle. Not
that she would have appeared to him pictorially
or in the imagination. It was more like the hint
of a figure he had seen inwardly days before,
like the perception of a form in the distance
when one sees an outline and colours and
recognises the expression on the face. She was
smiling and comforted him: 'I am with you,
because you are missing the Mother (Teresa). I

am your Mother.' This helped him somewhat, but he could not stop imagining Angela to himself and thinking of her and praying that God would take her into his glory.

Eventually the Sisters too found out what had happened. He comforted them as best he could, telling them that Angela was now happy in God and could rest, and would care for her Sisters from eternity even more than before, then he went to sleep in a state of deep sorrow and despondency. After he had been asleep for a short while he woke up abruptly with a heavy head, but he could not manage to get up. As he lay there in this state, he thought he saw his Angela very close to him and looking cheerful. Not that she appeared as in a vision or in his imagination, but he sensed her presence like that of the Holy Virgin earlier. Angela had come, and he formed an inward picture of her when she spoke to him: 'I am not far away. We will always walk together, and now I can really help you, Eliseo, for you are detached from everything and are part of Angela.' 'Pass on your virtues to me, for I am responsible for the souls of your daughters', said Eliseo, and at once the desire came over him to change his name and start calling himself 'Jerónimo de Jesús'. He immediately felt the presence of his Divine Mother smiling warmly at him, and Angela and Christ smiled along with her, they seemed to be enjoying themselves as if they were joking.

Then Eliseo's mind was overwhelmed by the greatness of his sins, and it terrified him that Angela now knew all about him. He trembled and felt like sinking into the ground for shame at the thought that Angela could henceforth see all the evil in him. He spent many hours in an intense state of repentance and penitence, wanting to please Angela and wanting to be worthy to speak with her. Still in this state of mind he got up early before dawn, for both calmness and sleep were eluding him. Throwing himself down before the crucified Christ, he sensed that Angela was kneeling next to him. The Holy Virgin came over and smiled at him, but he was embarrassed and afraid on account of how close to him Angela was. Yet it seemed to him that they were saying together: 'Don't worry! We are both very close to you.' Then he again asked Jesus and the Holy Virgin and Angela if he could inherit her virtues, which he needed so much. Soon a joyful confidence filled him that his plea would be granted.

These virtues that he craved included: living constantly in the presence of Christ and enjoying his presence in the soul so that he never leaves it whether or not the soul is aware of him; prayer leading to powerful and supernatural effects; growth in love; boundless obedience; deep humility without the temptation to boast about it; freedom from scruples arising from great purity of soul; joy at having brought others to God; a yearning to serve the Lord; adoration of the Holy Spirit together with an honouring of our dear Lady and Saint Joseph; patience in sufferings and trials; transparency of soul and capacity for spiritual discernment, openness and cheerful naturalness. Eliseo had discerned these and many other gifts in Angela. He felt that Angela did want to bequeath them to him so that he could pass them on to all her daughters.

Later on that morning Eliseo once again focussed his mind on the decision that had always been his permanent bedrock: always to strive to do what was most pleasing to God. He had already given a firm promise about this to Angela. Now it was the day before All Saints Day and Eliseo celebrated a high Mass. When he reached the eucharistic memorial after the consecration, Angela came up to him again and the Holy Virgin was with her. The two of them induced Eliseo to repeat his vow before the crucified Christ.

In the afternoon of that day I (*sic*) was recalling some of the merrily childish little things we would get up to together. Then such a feeling of tenderness welled up in me that I found myself giving free rein to my tears, and there was a sweetness in the memories that has remained with me ever since, even now that the tears have run dry.

On the same day I heard confessions in the convent. Wanting to continue to work together with her in all matters connected with the Order, I called out to her, and it was as though she took her place next to me on the bench. She was amused that the heavenly perspective on our imperfections was so different from the earthly. We can be so mistaken about them. But I felt dejected and lamented that my wretchedness and imperfections disqualified me from being a judge in such sensitive matters. At the same time I kept on asking God to help me and enlighten me. Then the Sisters came and confessed their sins, while I listened even more attentively to what the one I had at my side seemed to be saying about them.

She demonstrated the great connections that
could be made between each and every little sin
of the nuns and provided me with numerous
explanations which cannot be listed here.

That night I recalled our time together in Beas
and Angela's decision at that point to pledge
obedience to me. This made me feel bold
enough to call out to her and insist that she
support us, even though she was in heaven.
Now I found I could say anything to her that I
had on my heart just as openly and naturally as
before. So I lay down and went on discussing
all our business with her, giving her an account
of how things stood just as if I had travelled to
see her in Avila and been together with her
there as in the past. I recall speaking quite freely
and even loudly, and it seemed to me that she
and the Holy Virgin were smiling at all my
troubles. But I boldly refused to let go of her
hand until I went to sleep. She and the holy
Virgin remained by my side, each on one side
of my bed. Never in my life would I have dared
to show my thankfulness to Our Dear Lady in
any other way than by moving closer to her
hand, and even that only tremblingly, where-
upon my soul fell into a state of deep exhaustion. The same thing happened to me with
Angela. I say that because I had already gone
to bed and she could not look any different to
me from what she had done in life. Only with
Christ is a perfect union possible in the depths
of the soul.

On the morning of All Saints day Eliseo asked
Angela never to depart from his side, for her
presence comforted him so much! She
answered: 'As long as you do not separate

yourself from God, Eliseo, I will be with you too because I am constantly united with Him.' He said: 'You know *Madre mia*, that I was often afraid when you lived in this world, and you also know how I trembled before you if I fell into temptation, since I suspected even then that you saw right through me and knew my motivations. But now when it is quite certain that you see all that I do, my fear and my reverence are even more justified. Most of all I have always been afraid of my thoughtlessness, the root of all my failings. If you see this in me, then I beg you to warn me Angela, for I am very careless and feckless.

At the hour of afternoon prayer Eliseo recalled how happy Angela had always been when he helped her to pray it in Latin. They liked to speak the verses together, and it had been gratifying for Eliseo to see how well Angela understood them and prayed them. Now she could do for him what he once had done for her, namely explain these texts. She also warned him to exercise rather more severity in the fulfilment of his office. This would be easier for him if he made a practice of constantly meditating on God's commandments. Then, even had he a thousand lives, he would prefer to give everything up rather than to see a single one of these commandments broken. Likewise he was not to allow anyone to overstep or alter the rules and statutes of the Order. She also told him that she recognised very clearly now that she enjoyed eternal happiness what was the real goal of all the strivings for perfection, the foundations of monasteries, and the visitations of Eliseo; it was always a matter of love for God and neighbour, and he must make it his business to see to it that love of God grew in the newly-founded houses together with love of neighbour and that peace reigned. Even though there would always be things that could be improved, slanders and accusations must never be tolerated, since they grew out of rancour and aversion. Finally Angela also gave the reason why she had gone up to heaven, and she comforted Eliseo very much in doing so. She said: 'I was no more use in the world because I had grown old and tired and could not stay in all of the houses. Therefore the heavenly bridegroom took me to himself for ever. I am happy here now and I am joyfully united with him and feel present in each of my convents as the Mother of numerous children, and my daughters do so much good, remembering me.' — LAUS DEO.

Notes

1 *Letters* ii, 838 no 366, 24 May 1581.
2 *Letters* ii, 667 no 281, 24 June 1579.
3 *Letters* ii, 670 no 282, 7 July 1579.
4 *Letters* ii, 806 no 349, 17 Feb 1581.
5 Translator's note: Perceval was a knight connected in Medieval poetry with the legend of the quest for the Holy Grail.
6 *Letters* ii, 839 no 366, 24 May 1581.
7 *Letters* ii, 840 no 366, 24 May 1581.
8 *Letters* ii, 899 no 395, 4 Dec 1581.
9 *Foundations* ch. 31, xvi in *CW* iii, 292.
10 *Letters* ii, 965 no 434, 1 Sept 1582.
11 *Letters* ii, 716 no 305, 14 Jan 1580.
12 *Interior Castle* VII, ix in *CW* ii, 436.
13 *Spiritual Testimonies* 65, i-ix in *CW* i, 363-5.
14 In: *Revista de Archivos, Bibliotecas y Museos*, Madrid, 1913. 'Diálogo de un pastor y una pastora sobre el govierno de

zierto ganado. Sattiavor cum apperuerit Gloria tua. Diálogo de Angela y Heliseo desde 22 ottubre de 1582'. The editor, Juan Menéndez Pidal, found the MS, an extract from the 16th century, together with letters and autobiographical fragments 'of the persecuted and calumniated P. Jerónimo' among the treasures of the Archivo Nacional Histórico, the State Historical Archives.

7

THE SUFFERINGS OF ANASTASIO

Thunder and Doria[1]

ITH THE ORDER Chapter held in Almodóvar on 1 May 1583, dark clouds began to gather over the head of Father Jerónimo Gracián, confirming the fears felt by Teresa at the end of her life. Doria publicly reproached him for having inflicted great damage on the Order by his lax leadership of it. But when the angry Assembly wanted to remove their Provincial without more ado, Doria then took up his defence. Was his initial thunder just a matter of histrionics? The crucial point is that it was now quite evident which of them had the greater prestige in the Congregation, for a Provincial who owed his position to Doria was a weakened Provincial.

Continuing to behave with his usual generosity and friendliness, Gracián went his way unconcerned. He was mainly preoccupied with the idea of mission, a subject on which he had absorbed Teresa's thinking: this concern corresponded to his inclination for practical activity on a worldwide basis. He would have liked to save 'billions' of souls (Teresa only spoke of millions), and thus on 19 March 1582 — at the time of the foundation of Burgos in fact — with the consent of the Mother of the Order he had drawn up the first authorisation document for 'discalced' Carmelite missionaries. They were to go both to Ethiopia and to the countries of the Gulf of Guinea, known at the time simply as the Slave Coast and the Ivory Coast. Gracián loathed slavery of any kind and wanted to help blacks as well as whites. A small group of fathers was thus instructed to avail themselves of 'the next opportunity for embarkation'. At the same time the document allowed for the possibility of further missions 'anywhere in heathen lands', so that soon America too was included: first of all Mexico, later Peru and Chile.

In Christian Europe the Congregation of the Discalced soon possessed substantial convents in Italy and Portugal and the Order spread quickly in France, Belgium, and the German-speaking world. Gracián had hopes of pushing forward from foundations in Poland as far as Moscow. All this of course after the death of Teresa. Her highly-placed Calced enemy, Father Tostado, ensured that Portugal, so near from every point of view, remained out of bounds for a while. His name gave Spain's greatest baroque lyric poet, Luis de Góngora y Argote, the occasion for a frivolous-reverential poem, in which he pressed a play on words involving the 'roasted one' (Tostado) and the 'smoked one' (Ahumada), and another involving physical feet and metrical feet in relation to the Discalced (i.e. literally 'shoeless') Teresa. In the Baroque era people were very aware of the battles in the Order as they were of Teresa's canonisation. Another great man of the period, Francis of Sales—translated into Spanish by Quevedo—admired Teresa's example as a spiritual Christian when she submitted in obedience to Father Gracián:

'Happy the obedient', translated Quevedo, 'for God never allows them to go aside from the way and get lost'. Events in the Order were making great waves.

Gracián's social involvement also moved and inspired not only his contemporaries but also later generations. After Portugal fell to the Spanish crown in 1580 there were all kinds of conspiracies and rebellions. Father Jerónimo worried a great deal about the political prisoners who were the casualties of all this, and wanted the two countries to make an agreement about them. But above all it was women who were the main recipients of his love and care. Our Blessed Lady and Holy Mother Teresa had set their mark on his soul.

Teresa on the other hand had not been happy when an excessive emphasis on social activism threatened to jeopardise the contemplative heart of her reform. It was not until after her death that in Lisbon Gracián founded a house for the recovery and rehabilitation of women who had been brutalised by soldiers; later he founded a kind of convent for repentant prostitutes in Naples as well.

However, the very first thing that made enemies for him in the Order was his passion for the missions. When his term of duty ran out and the Chapter gathered in Lisbon, he himself suggested his archenemy Doria as his successor. John of the Cross remarked: 'He chose the one who would one day rob him of his habit'. Gracián was then immediately sent away from Spain to be Provincial Vicar of Portugal, where he became Prior in Lisbon. From there in 1586 he published a highly combative piece 'On the necessity of the spread of the faith'. In it he suggested that all the Orders should collaborate in world mission, and he indulged in polemic against his opponents among the Discalced with powerful arguments taken from the words of Christ and the example of the Apostles. He reproached the friars for an attitude that wanted to do

mission work only in Europe or only through prayer;
this he dismissed as a subtle achievement of the devil.
He did not shrink from complaining that while people
were perfectly ready to risk the journey to America for
the purposes of the trade in cowhide, they would
resolutely refuse to take their own skin to market for
the sake of Christ. The number of his enemies in his
own ranks grew to be 'legion', and yet he himself
persisted with his style of leadership in Portugal—
seemingly (if it were possible) more carefree than ever.
At the same time he fought against sectarianism and
made a name for himself with the unmasking of some
of the large number of false saints whose emergence
had been encouraged by the fashion of the time. In
cheerful broken Portuguese he related in his autobiography how through his intervention a famous stigma-
tist 'was freed from her wounds with warm water and
soap'.

His cheerfulness could not however dispel the
distant rumbles of thunder which now gathered and
finally broke over his head. At the end of his Spanish
period of office he had attempted a rather weak
apologia. In it he says bitterly:

> Anyone entrusted with the office of governing
> the Order must have a great deal of patience.
> He will have a long battle with himself to accept
> that all the efforts in the world on his part will
> be rewarded merely with slanders and ingrati-
> tude. If he does not direct his hopes solely
> towards heaven, there will be nothing left in the
> end for him but sorrow and dejection.

His opponent, Doria, fought with his own weapons.
Doria had the King practically in his pocket, since he
had helped him out of severe financial difficulties at a

time when Philip II was sliding from one state bank-
ruptcy to another. The prudent Genoan had won over
the Pope in the course of his long stay in Rome (which
Gracián himself had of course prescribed for him).
Now he began to make the most meticulous prepara-
tions for the first General Chapter, due to take place
on 19 June in Madrid. He succeeded in gaining authorisation for the expulsion of rebellious friars from the
Order, and he also acquired a Brief from Pope Sixtus
V which confirmed the new form of Administration
by a 'Consulta' ('Senate') which he desired to put in
place.

The Order had meanwhile grown to 60 monastic
houses with about 2000 members, so since Teresa's
death it had multiplied fourfold. Friars were still in the
majority over nuns. The saint had already made a point
of saying that the Order as a whole could no longer be
administered by one individual on his own. But the
Brief of Pope Sixtus could be interpreted in different
ways, and the Discalced almost split: Gracián understood it to mean that the seven-headed 'Consulta' had
an advisory rather than a governing role. For Doria by
contrast the whole point of it was to attribute an
absolute power of rule to this committee. On the one
hand no individual was to be sole ruler any more—for
he equated Gracián's patriarchal style of governance
with arbitrary tyranny—while on the other hand
everything 'democratic'—i.e. in accord with Teresa's
wishes—was eliminated. The Consulta was, as Gracián
demonstrated, a kind of elitist-aristocratic-led republic
on the pattern of Genoa or Venice. In Doria's scheme
all the power was in the hands of a small, tight, and
centralised ruling 'Council'. The monasteries would
no longer be allowed to choose their priors, while the

nuns would no longer be allowed to discuss their inner
difficulties with a familiar Father Provincial but must
submit them to an alien committee of seven men (six
'Councillors' and the General Vicar), whose discus-
sions would inevitably turn trivia into matters for legal
dispute.

That Gracián would be up in arms against this form
of governance was to be foreseen, for it stripped the
members of the Order of rights that had been absolutely sacred to Teresa. When he submitted a formal
complaint to Rome, this simply set the final seal on
Doria's hatred for him. At first Doria wanted to be rid
of him 'amicably', planning to dispatch him to Mexico
as Provincial Vicar. At the same time he was gathering
a wealth of accusations from all who felt resentment
against Father Jerónimo. To us today they look like
petty and distorted niggles whose emptiness is trans-
parent. Gracián reduced their overheated core to a
simple remark: '*Monjas!*' (Nuns!).

But at that time the accusations were dangerous and
Gracián, who after initially wavering eventually
decided he did not want to go to Mexico, saw himself
forced to compose a humble letter of apology. He
wrote it six weeks before the opening of the General
Chapter in Madrid, which went on to choose Doria as
Vicar General on 18 June 1588. Gracián was badly
advised with this letter. In it he stressed (in vain as it
transpired) that he had never knowingly done anything bad, even though he might have made mistakes
through thoughtlessness; he (equally vainly)
renounced all desire for office, expressing the hope
that he could enjoy the calm of a monastery designated
for him, somewhere where he could devote himself to

intellectual labours after so many years of relentless activity.

It was all too easy for Doria to interpret every sentence as an acknowledgement of guilt.

The General Chapter decided that the only place they could accommodate Gracián was Mexico, but he refused to go, and he did everything on his side to prove the illegality of the 'Consulta'. The conflict reached an unbearable pitch. Doria's collection of accusations grew 'convincingly'. Gracián's friends— among them John of the Cross and Fray Luis de León, the spiritual leader of the Spanish Renaissance who published Teresa's Works in 1588—supported his cause in vain. His expulsion was agreed on.

Father Jerónimo gave the impression of a hunted hare whose numerous darting manoeuvres in the face of the pitiless drive of the hunt merely made the end the more certain. In 1591 he wrote: 'There is neither hope nor help'. He did not recognise the competence of the Consulta, which wanted to force him to confessions that were as humiliating as they were untrue (pressure was even exerted in the confessional). So he could be condemned as 'unteachable', a charge that carried with it the right to exclude someone from the Order. The document was signed on 17 February 1592 under Doria's chairmanship in Madrid.

Slave of the Turks

A broken Jerónimo Gracián went first of all to stay with his widowed mother, formerly a close friend of the great Teresa. In the following year the Discalced Congregation achieved the status of an independent Order, but without Teresa's favourite comrade-in-arms and first Provincial. However, Gracián's long-

repressed fighting spirit had in the meantime rea-
woken. He travelled to Rome with the aim of obtaining
redress, only to be shown the door there.

After travels in Southern Italy and a period of
reflection, he determined to make a second attempt in
Rome and embarked on a galley of the Inquisition from
Sicily, which was to take him to Naples. Shortly before
it reached its destination—now said to be on 11
October 1593—Turks with their sailboats attacked the
ponderous vessel and took the Christians prisoner. The
galley-slave of the Turks was taken off towards Africa.
The priest, now clothed in little more than a pair of
handcuffs, had to sleep below decks on shotguns, (a
powder keg as a pillow'. He was made to clean the
weapons with the pages of the manuscript he was
taking to Rome to be printed—it was an important
work.

When a storm threatened, the vessel landed on an
idyllic island. While Gracián was sunk in quiet medi-
tation there, a Turk came up with a red hot iron and
burnt a cross onto the sole of his right foot. Calmly
Jerónimo of the Mother of God held out his left foot
too. Was he perhaps thinking of Teresa then? She
wrote in her *Interior Castle*—so familiar to him: 'Do you
know what it means to be truly spiritual? It means
becoming the slaves of God. Marked with His brand,
which is that of the cross, spiritual persons, because
they have given Him their liberty, can be sold by Him
as slaves of everyone, as He was.'[2]

The Turks had been hoping that this 'insult' to a
Christian priest would be a way of gaining them
favourable winds, and the winds certainly did improve
for them. They soon landed on the Tunisian coast,
where Gracián was sold as a slave at auction in Bizerte.

Yet neither hunger, nor having to work in foot irons, nor the threat of death by fire robbed him of his faith, his love, or his hope, nor his winning humour. Undaunted, the sympathetic and gently heroic man evangelised cowardly Christians and brave Turks. The Turks, who considered him to be a candidate for the Holy See and 'called him *Papaz*, just as we say 'Reverend Father', soon thought that such an illustrious prisoner should be sent as a gift to Constantinople to the Grand Turk himself, who had had a big cage built to hold just such persons.

Gracián feared he would now be imprisoned 'like a bird in this cage' to the end of his days. But fortunately the Pasha in Turkey took an interest in this slave, who had been brought to him with a great entourage of sabres and rifles. The Pasha soon came to treasure and protect the friendly man, although at one point he was again threatened with death by fire when they wrongly identified him as an Inquisitor. This imprisonment lasted for eighteen months, with the chains becoming literally heavier and heavier. Then came salvation in the shape of a Jew. Father Gracián had saved a relative of his in Lisbon from certain death. Able to scrape the required sum together only with great difficulty, the Jew nonetheless purchased him. The whole business was very dramatic at the time, but later Gracián liked to laugh at his 'value' of 1300 Escudos in gold. In a letter of 1601 he remarked that his price must in the meantime have gone up to 2000, since he had now made new acquaintances who valued him.

The purchase of his freedom in Tunis was completed on 11 April 1595. Gracián went via Genoa to Rome and threw himself at the feet of the Pope. He

wanted to return to his Order, the Discalced Carmelites. Pope Clement VIII soon became his friend and
was keen to help him. And Doria had died one year
earlier.

But under their new General the Discalced persisted
so resolutely in their resistance that the Pope gave up
and convinced Gracián that it would be better to go to
the 'Calced' of the mitigated observance. The latter
welcomed him very warmly into their priory in Rome.
Again Father Jerónimo saw a word of St Teresa fulfilled, for as early as 1579 she had virtually recommended him to move over to the Calced on account of
the danger he was facing.

The Pilgrim journey of life

Reflecting in Rome on the course of his life, Gracián
felt that it had been spent on a great world stage where
he had had to do a penance involving changing his
costume more often than an actor.

> My first costume had been the solemn robe of
> a university teacher. This was followed by the
> coarse woollen habit of the Discalced Car-
> melites, patched and dirty. When they threw
> me out of the Order, they put me in the most
> blessed uniform of the secular priest, which I
> exchanged for the gown of the pilgrim hermit,
> with a big hat over my monk's tonsure. That's
> how I was dressed to go to Rome. But when I
> became a prisoner, I wore a black woollen habit
> and a similar cloak without a hood, for I was
> already thinking of joining the barefoot Augus-
> tinians. Whereupon God gave me the clothing
> in which he had made me and I saw myself
> more or less naked, with hardly a shred to cover
> me. Then I found myself in coarse rags again,

with a little blue cap and torn shoes. When I
was taken to Tunis, I wore blue and red striped
cotton flannel. Soon after I was clothed all in
white, with a small scapular and boots into
whose tops the iron chains could be fastened.
Along with a little round cap on my head like
the Jews wear. After I was ransomed I dressed
in white cotton with the brown cape of the
galley slave, along with that mark of the freed-
man—a cross round my neck and a hat.

Then I put on a black- and white- striped cape
which I had brought with me from Barbary.
When I came to Rome with my request for
reinstatement, I was clothed in a fine black cloak
and similar cassock, marking me out as a priest
who had escaped from the Turks. Equipped
with a papal document (Brief), I was expecting
to be able to resume my old Discalced habit, but
they clothed me in that of the Calced instead—
which many pious and learned men in this
Order have worn. So then there was no more
reason for me to wander around as a penitent.

Soon he was taken on as secretary and theological
adviser in his Roman house by Cardinal Beza, who
had jurisdiction over Spain. But his tireless creative
energies still found opportunity for an outlet in his
own writings—and especially in his work on the
Italian edition of the Works of Teresa.

He was sent off again by Pope Clement VIII and the
new King Philip III on a missionary commission to
Africa. From time to time he stayed in different
Spanish monasteries of the Calced Carmelites in order
to write books and get them printed as part of his
apostolate. Not until 1607 did his wanderings come to
an end when he accepted an invitation to Brussels,

where he was to give spiritual oversight from a base in the Carmelite monastery to prominent personalities from the Court. However in this monastery of attenuated observance he lived a rather isolated life, since they spoke Flemish, so he concentrated on his works and memoirs. Looking back, he wrote in the 'Pilgrimage of Anastasio', completed shortly before his death: 'Suffice it to say that Mother Teresa gave me advice, encouragement, and comfort—for the rest, the less said, the better.'

In April 1614 he had the joy of experiencing her beatification by Pope Paul V. Five months later he was laid low by a short and painful illness which presaged the end of his days on 21 September. His desire to die in the habit of the Discalced was not fulfilled, still less his wish to found a monastery on Mount Carmel. It is said that on his deathbed he murmured verses by Teresa.

He was buried amid great demonstrations of respect in the Brussels monastery chapel.

Madrid too remembered him in a memorial ceremony ordered by the Court. In the Carmelite church the celebrated preacher Magister Fray Andrés de Lezana said that Father Jerónimo of the Mother of God had won the martyrs' crown. He went on to speak of the trust that holy Mother Teresa had shown in Gracián, and in so doing he jumped four centuries to style her a Doctor of the Church. We ought therefore, he argued, to give serious reflection to the fact that she submitted in freely-willed obedience to her young Provincial Jerónimo Gracián, especially given that they both chose to bind themselves to a vow of perfection. He was, the preacher said in his eulogy, truly a new Elishah, disciple and heir of a woman who could be seen as the new Elijah. The holy bond between the two prophets in the divine fire made of them 'two loving Seraphim flying down from God and going back to God. The flight of the holy Mother and the flight of this man sent from God was just like that.' Teresa's love, he continued, was not blind, for she was a seer whose visions were fulfilled, and ultimately we could now say of the one who had just passed away: 'His is the victory'.

Five days before his death, while he was still well, Gracián wrote about his plan to make a collection of the poems written on the beatification of Teresa and publish it. On the next day he spoke in a letter to his brother about the heavenly Jerusalem, the goal of all life's journeys, to which he felt—God be praised—already near!

He may have imagined it as peaceful and shining in the way it was portrayed in the verses which Cervantes wrote in 1614 in Alba de Tormes on the death of St Teresa—taking the word 'alba' symbolically as 'daybreak':

Born in Avila
You came to life in Alba,
The life that will be given in dying
To those who have chosen God.

You climb, Mother, into the pure
Morning radiance in eternal beauty,
You will not deny us too
Love, which reconciles us to God.

Your humility, much praised,
Has won heaven for you,
And there humility can do all,
Draw us poor souls up there!

Notes

1   The quotation from Schiller's 'Fiesko' [translator's note: *in which the phrase 'Donner und Doria' occurs*] relates to Andrea Doria from another Genoan family of the same century.

2   *Interior Castle* VII:4, viii in *CW* ii, 446.

BIBLIOGRAPHY[1]

Teresa de Jesús, *Obras completas*. Biblioteca de Autores Cristianos, Madrid 1977. Quotations from:

Vida (Life); *Cuentas de Conciencia* (Reports of inner experience), *Camino de Perfección* (Way of Perfection), *Libro de las Fondaciones* (Book of Foundations), *Meditaciones sobre el Cantar de Cantares* (Meditations on the Song of Songs), *Visita de Descalzas* (On making the visitation), *Las Moradas del Castillo interior* (The interior Castle), *Epistolario* (Letters), *Exclamaciones* (Soliloquies).

P. Jerónimo Gracián de la Madre de Dios, *Obras*, 3 vols, Biblioteca Mistica Carmelitana, Burgos 1932-33. Quotations from:

Vol 1: *Dilucidario del verdadero espiritu* (On the true spirit = Defence and explanation of the work of Teresa).

Vol 2: *Sermones* (Sermons): *Declamacion en que se trata de la perfecta vida y virtudes heróicas de la beata Madre Teresa de Jesús y de las fundaciones de sus monasterios.* (Address on the perfect life and heroic virtues of the blessed Mother Teresa de Jesús, and on her foundations of convents).

Vol. 3: *Celo de la propagación de la Fe* (On the necessity of the spread of the faith). *Tratado de la Redención de Cautivos* (Treatise on the Redemption of captives). *Peregrinación de Anastasio*: (see 1st ed. 1905). *Epistolario* (Letters 1572-1614). *Avisos acerca del gobierno* (Counsels about the governance of the Order). *Patente de los primeros Misioneros Descalzos a Guinea e instrucciones par la Misión* (Patent for the first Discalced Carmelites for the Guinea mission with instructions). Appendix: *Sermón que predicó el P. M.*

Andrés de Lezana (Sermon at the memorial service for Jerónimo de Gracián in Madrid).

Id., *Peregrinación de Anastasio* (The pilgrimage of Anastasio, autobiography), El Monte Carmelo, Burgos, 1905.

Id., *Diálogos sobre la muerte de la M. Teresa de Jesús* (Dialogues on the death of Mother Teresa of Jesus), El Monte Carmelo, Burgos, 1913.

Id., *Scholias y Addiciones al Libro de la vida de la Me Theresa de Jesús que compuso el Pe Doctor Ribera. Hechas por fray Gmo de la madre de Dios Carmelita descalço* (Marginal notes and additions by Fr Jerónimo de la Madre de Dios OCD to the Book of the Life of Mother Teresa of Jesus, edited by Fr Dr Ribera) in: *El Monte Carmelo* Nr. 68, 1960, pp. 99-165.

Id., *Diálogo de Angela y Heliseo desde 22 de octubre de 1582: Diálogo de un pastor y una pastora sobre el govierno de zierto Ganado* (Dialogue between Angela and Eliseo on 22 October 1582; Dialogue of a shepherd and a shepherdess about the leading of a certain flock), in: *Revista de Archivos*, Bibliotecas y Museos, 1913, pp. 93-100. (Ed. J. Menéndez Pidal).

Id., *Regla primitive y constituciones de las monjas descalças de la Orden de nuestra Señora la virgin María del monte Carmelo*, Salamanca 1581. *A la muy religiosa Madre Teresa de Jesús, fundadora de los monasterios de las monjas Carmelitas Descalças.* (Original rule and principles of the Discalced nuns of the Order of our Dear Lady of Mount Carmel. To the reverend Mother Teresa de Jesús, foundress of the Discalced Carmelite convents), in: *Obras de Santa Teresa de Jesús*, VI. Biblioteca Mistica Carmelitana, Burgos, 1919, Appendix pp. 409ff. Here also the statement of Pope Gregory XIII on the erection of their own province for the Discalced and similar documents from the years 1575-1581.

María de San José, *Fundación del convento de Carmelitas Descalças en Sevilla, y persecuciones que padecieron hast la época de la muerte de Sant Teresa*, (Foundation of the convent of Discalced Carmelites in Seville, and report on the persecutions under which all in the time down to the death of St Teresa had to suffer), in: *Escritos de Santa Teresa, añadidos e ilustrados por don Vicente de la Fuente*, tomo II, Madrid 1862, Biblioteca de Autores Españoles pp. 555-561. In this volume also documents on the death of Gracián and letters of the General of the Order Rubeo to St Teresa. In vol. I of the same edition report of Gracián on the obedience of Teresa and important Patents (full powers) of the General.

Aelred of Rievaulx, *On Spiritual Friendship* (mid-twelfth century), tr. Mary Eugenia Laker SSND, Kalamazoo: Cistercian Publications, 1977.

P. Efrén de la M. de Dios OCD y P. Otger Steggink OC, *Tiempo y Vida de Santa Teresa*, revised ed., Madrid 1977.

P. Otger Steggink OC, *Erfahrung und Realismus bei Teresa von Avila und Johannes vom Kreuz*, Patmos, Düsseldorf, 1976.

P. Silverio de Santa Teresa OCD, *Historia del Carmen Descalzo en España, Portugal y America*. 15 vols., vol. VI Gracián/Doria, El Monte Carmelo, Burgos 1937. With documentation in an appendix, including Gracián's Defence against slanders (not in the Obras).

Erika Lorenz, *Teresa von Avila: Ich bin ein Weib und obendrein kein gutes*, Herderbücherei 920, Freiburg i.Br. 1982.

Id., *Francisco de Osuna, Versenkung*, Herbderbücherei 938, Freiburg 1982.

Id., *Ein Karmelit als Türkensklave*, in: *Geist and Leben*, Dez. 1982.

Miguel de Cervantes, *Los Éxtasis de la Beata Madre Teresa de Jesús*, in: *Compendio* etc., (Collection of poems for the Beatification), ed. Diego de San José, 1615.

Luis de Góngora y Argote, *En la Beatificación de Santa Teresa*,
Góngora submitted this poem, which has both a cheerful
and also a serious note, to a lyric poetry competition on
the occasion of the beatification of Teresa in Córdoba.
He won a pair of black silk stockings.

Francisco de Quevedo, Spanish Translation of the *Introduc-
tion to the devout life* by St Francis de Sales.

The Chronicler named in the foreword is Francisco de Santa
María (Pulgar y Sandoval) OCD, Reforma de los Descal-
zos de Nuestra Señora del Carmen de la primitive
Observancia, Madrid 1644-1655, 2 vols.

Not cited, but important for the spiritual horizon, was the
book by J. Bours and J.Kamphaus, *Leidenschaft für Gott*,
Herder, Freiburg, 1981.

Gracián's brother Tomás composed the following
poem for Gracián:

The painter shows on this picture
Persecuted goodness without guilt,
Suffering, borne in patience.
Perfection, great mildness
Pardons what evil plots.
Slander, lies, ambition, envy:
They were ready to oppress
The noble: God gave their works
Free rein, since they strengthen in the pious
The stream of grace of holiness.

Notes

[1] I am grateful to the Carmelite convents in Würzburg and
Mariazell, whose friendly patience procured me the loan of
a great part of the material here listed.

www.ingramcontent.com/pod-product-compliance
Lightning Source LLC
Chambersburg PA
CBHW021059090426
42738CB00006B/414